BABY TROUBLE IN THE LAST BEST WEST

Making New People in Alberta, 1905–1939

Reproduction is the most emotionally complicated human activity. It transforms lives but it also creates fears and anxieties about women whose childbearing doesn't conform to the norm.

Baby Trouble in the Last Best West explores the ways that women's childbearing became understood as a social problem in early twentieth-century Alberta. Kaler utilizes censuses, newspaper reports, social work case files, and personal letters to illuminate the ordeals that women, men, and babies were subjected to as Albertans debated childbearing. Through the lens of reproduction, Kaler offers a vivid and engaging analysis of how colonialism, racism, nationalism, medicalization, and evolving gender politics contributed to Alberta's imaginative economy of reproduction. Kaler investigates five different episodes of "baby trouble": the emergence of obstetrics as a political issue, the drive for eugenic sterilization, unmarried childbearing and "rescue homes" for unmarried mothers, state-sponsored allowances for single mothers, and high infant mortality. *Baby Trouble in the Last Best West* will transport the reader to the turmoil of Alberta's early years while examining the complexity of settler society-building and gender struggles.

AMY KALER is a professor in the Department of Sociology at the University of Alberta.

T0323777

Baby Trouble
in the Last Best West

*Making New People in Alberta,
1905–1939*

AMY KALER

UNIVERSITY OF TORONTO PRESS
Toronto Buffalo London

© University of Toronto Press 2017
Toronto Buffalo London
www.utppublishing.com
Printed in Canada

ISBN 978-1-4426-4568-4 (cloth)   ISBN 978-1-4426-1394-2 (paper)

∞ Printed on acid-free, 100% post-consumer recycled paper with vegetable-based inks.

Library and Archives Canada Cataloguing in Publication

Kaler, Amy, 1966–, author
Baby trouble in the last best West : making new people in Alberta, 1905–1939 / Amy Kaler.

Includes bibliographical references and index.
ISBN 978-1-4426-4568-4 (hardback). – ISBN 978-1-4426-1394-2 (paperback)

1. Alberta – Social conditions – 1905–1945.   2. Reproductive rights – Alberta – History –
20th century.   3. Childbirth – Social aspects – Alberta – History – 20th century.
4. Human reproduction – Social aspects – Alberta – History – 20th century.   5. Women –
Legal status, laws, etc. – Alberta – History – 20th century.   6. Single mothers – Alberta –
Social conditions – 20th century.   7. Parenthood – Social aspects – Alberta – History –
20th century.   8. Illegitimacy – Alberta – History – 20th century.   9. Infants – Death –
Social aspects – Alberta – History – 20th century.   I. Title.

FC3672.9.R4K35 2017   971.23'02   C2016-905917-0

University of Toronto Press acknowledges the financial assistance to its
publishing program of the Canada Council for the Arts and the Ontario Arts
Council, an agency of the Government of Ontario.

Canada Council   Conseil des Arts
for the Arts   du Canada

Funded by the   Financé par le
Government   gouvernement
of Canada   du Canada

Contents

Figures

Acknowledgments

I would like to acknowledge financial support from the Social Sciences and Humanities Research Council of Canada and the Killam Trust at the University of Alberta. I would also like to acknowledge research assistance by Ellen Whiteman, Randelle Nixon, and Sharon Springer. A portion of chapter 3 was previously published as part of "Treasures: Multiple Economies of Reproduction at the Beulah Rescue Home, Edmonton, Alberta, 1909–1963" in *Criminalized Mothers, Criminalizing Mothering*, edited by Joanne Minaker and Bryan Hogeveen, and published by Demeter Press in 2015. A portion of chapter 7 was previously published as part of "'The National Gain Is Nil': Talking About Infant Mortality in Interwar Alberta," in *Canadian Journal of Sociology* 38(3).

BABY TROUBLE IN THE LAST BEST WEST

Making New People in Alberta, 1905–1939

1 Introduction

Introduction

What would it mean for social history to take reproduction seriously? More precisely, what would it mean to put the reproduction of human beings at the centre of our stories about individual and collective continuity and change? In this book, I propose to do exactly that, by examining the making of new people in the first few decades of Alberta's existence, from 1905 to the beginning of the Second World War in 1939. I focus on "baby trouble": the complexities, anxieties, and difficulties that have characterized the social relations surrounding Albertan women's childbearing. "Baby trouble" incorporates the babies who were born under difficult or socially awkward circumstances; the women whose mothering made them into inconvenient subjects for the state; the men who took or did not take responsibility for these women and children; and the collective fears and strategies that were mustered up in response to the endless conundrums posed by human reproduction.[1]

This book proceeds as a series of episodes, each examining a different facet of "baby trouble." These episodes are organized thematically rather than strictly chronologically. In this introductory chapter, I bring in the ideas that have shaped my work, in particular, the concept of an imaginative economy of reproduction. The second chapter lays the groundwork regarding the social organization of reproduction by discussing the history of childbirth as an institutionalized phenomenon in Alberta – that is, the physical, material conditions under which new people came into being. In the third chapter, we move into reproduction as troubled terrain as I discuss the issue of illegitimacy and the management of reproduction outside the normative framework of marriage through a case study of the principal home for unmarried mothers in Alberta.

The fourth chapter takes on the notorious Sexual Sterilization Act of 1927 by examining the parallel discursive streams of what I call "high" and "low" eugenics. The issue at hand was whether certain individuals or classes of people should be prohibited from reproduction. Racism and colonialism figured prominently in this debate, in that they animated fears about the "wrong" sort of people having babies.

The fifth chapter addresses the ways in which reproduction serves as a basis for claims-making and arguments about entitlement. I move beyond the events surrounding the biological creation of children to examine the controversies over whether lone mothers were entitled to allowances for raising children. Through these allowances, some women's reproductive actions were legitimized (i.e., if the women were widowed or had been deserted by a legal husband, or if their behaviour fell within socially approved bounds) while other types of actions were declared undesirable.

Finally, in the sixth chapter I discuss the ultimate form of troubled reproduction: infant mortality, the deaths of babies who had only just come into being. In framing infant mortality as a political problem, not simply a collection of individual tragedies, we see the imaginative economy of reproduction extended to encompass not only the making but also the unmaking of new people in Alberta.

The book's overall trajectory thus moves from the concrete and corporeal to the speculative and abstract. We begin by discussing the physical details of how babies got themselves born, then move through the social meanings attached to babies (and their mothers) as they embraced or strayed from idealized notions of proper reproduction, until we arrive, finally, at a consideration of babies who were never more than babies, the importance of whose lives to Alberta will never be known because they died soon after birth. In each chapter, I tell the story of a particular episode of baby trouble, but I also examine these episodes in the context of broader questions about reproduction in social theory. These questions differ by chapter: Is childbirth a political act (or a political duty)? Does welfare substitute for men in the lives of husbandless mothers? Is infant death a public tragedy? What political space can be claimed by the invocation of motherhood?

The Imaginative Economy of Reproduction

I start from the belief that reproduction is not merely a physiological process but "an ongoing social and political construction that begin[s] long before and continues long after the biological fact of parturition" (Bledsoe et al. 1994, 5). My inquiry is guided by two questions:

1. What kinds of reproduction have been defined as socially problematic (and conversely, socially desirable) in Alberta? What institutions and practices have been used to manage these socially problematic activities?
2. How have women's reproductive practices figured in the collective imagination of Albertans? In particular, how have they been linked to collective good of Alberta, both symbolically and materially?

This book is not just a story about who had children in Alberta at a particular time. It is also an extended account of what I call the *imaginative economy of reproduction* – the ways in which childbearing figures in how people think about themselves, individually and collectively, and the ways these meanings change over time. The imaginative economy approach also enables us to understand why reproduction has been differentially valued, depending on who is having the babies and the circumstances in which the babies are being born. The result is history with the messy parts left in, in which the physical and social struggles to make new people are just as important as the struggles around politics, economics, and culture, and indeed are part of those struggles.

This particular history is being written in concert with other scholars who have argued that the study of reproduction is not merely a side issue to the real business of studying society, but is (or should be) at the centre. The creation of new people through biological reproduction engages a vast array of social and political forces while simultaneously focusing those forces on a finite set of human practices.

One of the first people to contend that reproduction is central to social life was Friedrich Engels, who made the sweeping claim that "the determining factor in history is ... the production and reproduction of immediate life ... on the one hand, the production of the means of subsistence, of clothes, food and shelter ... on the other, the production of human beings themselves, the propagation of the species" (qtd. in Ginsburg and Rapp 1991, 313). In their germinal review article, Faye

Ginsburg and Rayna Rapp argued that reproduction is key to state power and other forms of authority: "throughout history ... power has depended directly and indirectly on defining normative families and controlling populations" (315). They further asserted that reproduction is a key terrain in contestations for power, and they called for attention to "the ways in which these [reproductive processes] figure into understandings of social and cultural renewal" (318).

Similarly, Canadian sociologist Susan McDaniel (1996) assigns a central place to fertility and childbearing. She points out that reproduction, interpreted both as the material conditions under which people are born and as a metaphor for growth, continuity, and survival, is the pivot on which many debates in the social sciences turn. It follows that scholarship about reproduction is never merely about one discrete phenomenon in social life; indeed, if done well, it can illuminate much broader concerns. Viviana Zelizer's examination of the value, monetary and non-monetary, that has been assigned to intimate relationships such as between parent and child is one example of such work; Rickie Solinger's work on race, class, and "choice" as a trope in American political life is another; Lorna Weir's work on the making of unborn political subjects through the surveillance of pregnancy is yet another.

Although twenty years have gone by since scholars like McDaniel and Ginsburg and Rapp began to situate reproduction at the centre of social life, their views are still not mainstream in sociology, history, and anthropology (Roseneil et al. 2013). Nonetheless, in recent decades many scholars have placed reproduction at the heart of their investigations into the dynamics of nations and other institutions (e.g., Hiroko 2004; Paxson 2004; Schoen 2005; Kligman 1998; Kaaneh 2002; Gal and Kligman 2000; Bledsoe 2002; the contributors to Ginsburg and Rapp 1995). Most of them have adopted a "political economy of fertility" approach, which stresses the material conditions influencing who has how many babies under what circumstances. Demography too has moved towards more culturally nuanced studies (e.g., Greenhalgh 2008; Renne 2003; Bledsoe 2002; Schneider 1996); however, these studies tend to focus on fertility decline, a central preoccupation of demographers, but one that does not exhaust the imaginative power of reproduction.

In addition, Canadian sociologists and feminists have turned their attention to reproduction. Regional studies have been conducted by scholars such as Arnup (1994), Baillargeon (2009), Comacchio (1993), Chambers (2007), Levesque (1994), and Little (1998); and broader

Canadian theories of social reproduction have been developed by Luxton (1980), Bezanson and Luxton (2006), and Strong-Boag (2006, 2011). These scholars have taken up the "provocative [Marxist] assertion that social life is determined by both the production of the means of life and the propagation of the species" (Luxton 2006, 25) and have followed this trajectory to cast light on the complicated apparatus of incentives, constraints, and disciplines that have proliferated around the biological facts of producing and maintaining human life in Canada. Their historical work intersects with feminist political economy and Foucauldian cultural studies to produce multidimensional accounts of reproduction. Most of this scholarship has focused on the institutional contexts of reproduction, specifically the involvement of the Canadian state and other powerful actors in creating durable social relations that govern who gives birth and raises children under what circumstances. These institutions have influenced the division of household labour, the marginalization of unmarried mothers, the adoption and fostering of children, and the spread of child health interventions, and many other social developments.

Although I write about politics, economics, and certainly feminism, this book does not fit easily into the strong tradition of Canadian feminist political economy (Vosko 2002). That tradition, which took form in the 1970s through the work of scholars such as Marjorie Cohen, Bonnie Fox, Pat Armstrong, Meg Luxton, and Martha MacDonald, began with a critique of the gender-blindness of mainstream academic accounts of Canadian history. Their work, and the work of the scholars who followed them, focused on the entanglement of women's productive and reproductive labour. Questions of class, and of how class and gender were mutually constitutive, followed from these concerns. Canadian feminist political economy examined how capital and the state manifested themselves in women's everyday lives and how hierarchies (including, increasingly, hierarchies within processes of globalization) were sustained by gender inequity.

The role of social movements in remaking these social relations also came in for scrutiny, especially during the 1990s, when federal government cuts to women's advocacy organizations reverberated through the feminist movement. More recently, Canadian feminist political economy has focused on the intersections of gender with race, ethnicity, sexuality, and ability, and how women's (and men's) lives as gendered beings are shaped not just by the fact of being male or female, but by the interactions of multiple social categories, including but not limited to gender.

In this book, I take up some of the concerns raised by this tradition. I talk about the creation and circulation of value through women's work, and about women's interactions and negotiations with state agencies. I also examine the gendering of social change movements and women's advocacy work. The racism and xenophobia of a settler society forms a constant backdrop, manifesting itself strongly in some chapters and obliquely in others.

However, I move away from Canadian feminist political economy through my emphasis on imagination, meaning, and the ways that people talked about women's reproduction. The result is a book that may say more about culture than about political economy as it is usually conceived. That is why I use the phrase "imaginative economy of reproduction" and emphasize the notion of a social imaginary. Another writer, working with different data, might have told the stories of baby trouble as stories about class hierarchies and forms of production. However, the archival material I am working with here is more allusive and suggestive, giving rise to a landscape of how people thought about babies, women, and reproduction during some of Alberta's hardest years.

In this book, I extend these scholars' focus on the materiality of reproduction and the institutions through which it was managed to include the imaginative economy of reproduction – the ways in which people imagine and talk about childbearing in specific places and specific times. Through attention to the imaginative economy of reproduction, I illuminate how childbearing is imbued with the hopes, desires, fears, and aversions of both individuals and collective groups. This enables us to understand the significance of making new people both materially – in the production of humans, the essential ingredients of any society – and symbolically – as manifestations of valued or devalued ways of being and acting in the world. The imaginative economy approach also enables us to understand why reproduction has been differentially valued, depending on who is having the babies and the circumstances in which the babies are being born.[2]

The concept of an imaginative economy draws from the notion of a social imaginary. By "social imaginary," I mean the same thing as Charles Taylor when he differentiates between social theory and social imaginary:

I'm talking about the way ordinary people "imagine" their social surroundings, and this is often not expressed in theoretical terms ... It is also the case that theory is the possession of a small minority whereas what is interesting in the social imaginary is that it is shared by large groups, if not the whole of society. ... The social imaginary is that common understanding that makes possible common practices and a widely shared sense of legitimacy. (2002, 106)

As Taylor stresses, the social imaginary is not simply a layperson's version of social theories that describe the world; more importantly, is also that which brings certain practices into existence and excludes others. The social imaginary has powerful moral and normative components; it describes the way the world ought to be – and *could* be if some aspects of it were changed through human action – rather than simply the way the world is.

Imaginations and imaginaries are not simply abstract ideas about what is good and bad. They are powerful social forces that order the distribution of resources and the circulation of scarce and valuable products among people. For this reason, I have used the term "economy" to emphasize that I am talking not only about the ideas and understandings that proliferated in Alberta, but also about the practices and circulation of resources that went along with them.

Women, Men, and States

The imaginative economy of reproduction is founded on the sexed and gendered nature of human reproduction. Biologically, human reproduction requires the involvement of bodies that are generally considered to belong to two physical sexes, male and female. Socially, reproduction calls up the complexities of gender, which I here define as all those experiences, possibilities, constraints, and meanings associated with belonging to one sex or the other. Women produce babies, although not always in circumstances of their choosing. Men rely on women to produce these babies, but this need is never matched by the power to control women's reproduction, either to bring forth babies or to prevent them from being brought forth. (The heteronormativity of these relations, in their conventional form, is so pervasive as to be almost invisible.)

However, reproduction is not just a relationship between two categories, male and female. It is also an effect of the relations between these two kinds of people and the collectivities, such as communities, states, or societies, in which they live. In Alberta, this three-way relation

1.1 Women and children in a car, Wainwright, Alberta, before 1920.
Source: http://peel.library.ualberta.ca/postcards/PC005057.html

– men, women, collectivity – has situated childbearing as the *moral terrain of women, the contested responsibility of men, and the precarious necessity of the state.*

It follows that women are accorded moral valence by their childbearing. They are deemed ethically "good" or "bad" on the basis of their reproductive activities. As we will see throughout this book, a woman's status as "the mother," a moral figure, justifies her claims on individual men and on the state; that same status is used to justify restrictions or constraints placed on her. For men in early-twentieth-century Alberta, the fact that it was women who bore children, combined with the fact that men were much more powerful political and economic actors than women, meant that men often debated each other *and* with women over who should take responsibility for the care and support of women and children. Men in Alberta used their freedom to manoeuvre in order to evade, embrace, or reject the tasks of caring for dependent women and children, and to denounce other men for their behaviour in this regard, as will be demonstrated most clearly in chapter 5.

For the state, reproduction is a precarious necessity. To point out the obvious, states are comprised of people (or, in the words of Cynthia Comacchio [1993], nations are built of babies). The making of new people is a precondition for states, and unfortunately, the making of new people seldom runs smoothly. Women may have too few babies, or too many, or may have them at the wrong time or outside the conventional heterosexual dyad, causing moral consternation. As Roseneil and colleagues write, the good citizen is "properly procreative," that is, "procreative within the context of the co-residential, heterosexual, gender-normative couple" (2013, 903). We might add that in early-twentieth-century Alberta, the good citizen exercised oversight over procreation, having many children in some circumstances, few or none in others. Unfortunately, as this book shows, the orderly peopling of the state runs up against the messy contingencies of human behaviour. At times, as shown in chapter 6, the very existence of those babies is at risk.

Although reproduction is a dual-sexed and dual-gendered process, I focus primarily on one gender, women. Thus, a few words about the complex relations between women and the state are warranted. That women's citizenship – in a substantive if not a formal sense – is tied to their activities as reproducers is hardly a new insight. Roseneil and colleagues (2013) provide a good summary of the ways in which "reproductive citizenship" has been theorized. Women can be "good" citizens, who reproduce in accordance with the goals and interests of those who see themselves building a state, or they can be "bad" reproducers, whose actions are troublesome and troubling (Yuval-Davis and Anthias 1989; Yuval-Davis 1997). In this book I focus on the latter – indeed, this book is at heart a catalogue of the ways in which reproduction turned women into problems for the state in twentieth-century Alberta.

The state in question changed over the period under study, but it retained certain characteristics. Most importantly, it was a settler, colonial state, part of the European appropriation of North America. "Peopling" Alberta meant in practice providing a lot of white people plenty of geographic and social space to occupy, which meant displacing or disregarding the First Nations that were already there. As the title of chapter 2 states, white babies born in Alberta were "the little immigrant who comes into our homes," future citizens of the best kind. The term "white" itself was a floating signifier in early Alberta history, in that it could mean "descended from Europeans" in some settings, "English-speaking" in others, or simply "not one of the Others," where the Others were First Nations, Asians, Slavs, or any other Others. Women who could give birth to white babies were protected and encouraged for political reasons; women who gave birth to other babies (such as Aboriginal or Asian ones) might be the recipients of altruism or welfare initiatives, but they were not part of the nation-building project of white Alberta.

Besides being a settler state, Alberta was a masculine state (Carter 2008; Cavanaugh 1997). Although women gained the provincial franchise in 1916 (and the federal franchise in 1918), and women's organizations exercised considerable influence in policy areas considered suitable to them, such as child welfare, the decision-makers and wielders of authority were almost uniformly male. In the early twentieth century, the concerns of the Alberta government were largely the concerns of the traditionally masculine public sphere – gaining and holding geographic territory, establishing the rule of law, producing commodities to be bought and sold. As a consequence, public support for activities traditionally associated with the feminized private sphere, such as caring for children and dependents – or what Dorothy Smith calls the "everyday/everynight" activities of social reproduction – was almost non-existent (Smith 1999). Women were thus constantly having to petition the state and its men for resources and legitimacy, laying claim to money and support because of their status as reproducers. The chapters that follow describe some of the most complex of these contestations.

These complex relations gave rise to particular metaphors that run throughout all the chapters that follow. A major theme of this book is the predominance of certain metaphors or ways of speaking about reproduction. Mariana Valverde discovered that the purity and moral reform movements in English Canada relied on a shared vocabulary and set of images; in much the same way, I found recurrent analogies that shaped the imaginative economy of reproduction in Alberta (Valverde 2008). These are most visible in this book's final chapter, but their influence is evident in all the forms of baby trouble covered here.

The first analogy was between human reproduction and capitalistic economic activity. Metaphors of efficiency, profit, loss, gain, and waste were pervasive, with the birth of babies likened to the functioning of a profit-generating operation. If this operation functioned well, it was "profitable," for high-quality babies were born in an orderly fashion. If it did not function well, it resulted in a loss, for babies of poor quality appeared in a haphazard manner and did not provide good returns on public investments of money and resources. Babies were "stock," mothers were workers, and the state was either the investor or the owner, depending on the moment.

The second analogy was military. Perhaps it is not surprising that after the losses of the First World War, the concept of human reproduction as a battleground pervaded Alberta discourse. Babies (and mothers) were described variously as soldiers or as casualties on the battlefield of life, locked in struggle with physical, moral, or social antagonists. Making new people was not a peaceful process; it was a series of battles against forces that threatened either the quantity or the quality of Alberta's babies.

Why Alberta?

The term "Last Best West" was used by both the Canadian government and British immigration agents to describe Alberta: it was a frontier land where intrepid white settlers could flourish, thereby contributing to the building of the "best" society imaginable. For decades, Alberta has functioned in the Canadian political imaginary as a frontier, a place of risk and danger but also a place where the rules of the hidebound east do not apply, and where societies can, and must, be rebuilt along newer and better lines. Over the past century, Alberta has experienced waves of "prairie populism" that have been simultaneously conservative, libertarian, and reconstructionist. In the interwar years that are the focus of this book, Alberta had a successful woman suffrage movement, which was deeply bound up with the idea of collective betterment and thus overlapped with the concerns about infant mortality and "baby-saving" as well as with the repressive eugenic sterilization movement (see below).

As Canada's western frontier (politically, if not geographically), Alberta has carried out institutional practices and policies surrounding reproduction that have been more radical and often less regulated than anywhere else in Canada. Most notably, Alberta had the most extensive program of eugenic sterilization in North America, which did not end until 1972 (see chapter 4). Alberta's boom/bust economy over the past hundred years has swung repeatedly between giddy expansion and sharp contraction, and this has had dramatic consequences for childbearing. This makes it a prime untapped site for examining how "baby trouble" has been defined, managed, and tied to other social processes.

There have already been some excellent studies of various facets of reproduction in other regions of Canada, such as Comacchio (1993), Levesque (1994), Strong-Boag (2006), and Chambers (2007), but none of this work extends to the prairie West, where the political imperatives of white settlement and the "taming " of a frontier added extra

1.2 British recruitment poster for immigration to the "Last Best West."
Source: http://data2.archives.ca/ap/c/c030621.jpg

significance to reproduction. The published work that is closest to what I set out to do in this project is Sarah Carter's excellent book on marriage in the Canadian West (2008). However, Carter's work stops at the beginning of the twentieth century, roughly where mine starts, and focuses mainly on the legal and political questions surrounding the regulation of Aboriginal marriage.

In what is now Alberta from the beginning of the eighteenth century, whites and Native people had interacted through the fur trade. As Canada grew, Aboriginal lands became increasingly valuable to the Canadian government for purposes other than fur trapping, and Native people found themselves being restricted to parcels of land that had been set aside for Aboriginal reserves. In 1875, the federal North West Territories Act created an administrative jurisdiction out of the vast expanse of northwestern Canada. Before the act, the white presence in the area had been limited to fur trappers, traders, and missionaries; after it was passed, white settlers began arriving in increasing numbers on lands that had been obtained from the Native people through a series of treaties, many of which were of questionable legality. By then, the region's Aboriginal people were destitute as a result of disease, warfare, and the collapse of the buffalo herds. Most of the newcomers were farmers or ranchers. Under the Dominion Lands Act, any prospective settler could obtain a quarter-section (160 acres) of land simply by paying a $10 fee. Large tracts of land that had been reserved for the Canadian Pacific Railway were also up for grabs, with the CPR selling off its prime holdings next to the railways.

In the late nineteenth century, the government took steps to fill Alberta with white settlers. Canada needed the West's minerals and agricultural goods; and it also wanted to make sure the Americans didn't settle there first. Alberta was aggressively marketed to prospective immigrants in Britain and central Canada; marketing materials declared Alberta the "last best West," a place where good farmland was for the taking and where prosperity awaited the bold. In 1905, Alberta became a province, carved out of the Canadian West along with its neighbouring province, Saskatchewan. The stories this book tells start with that year and that event.

I focus on the early twentieth century, from the years immediately preceding the First World War to the outbreak of the Second World War. I had intended to write a sweeping history of reproduction in the twentieth century. However, it soon became clear that this would be an enormous task, given all the talking, thinking, and imagining of reproduction that had gone on in that hundred years. So I narrowed my focus to the interwar years, for several reasons. First, there was abundant archival material available. Second, Alberta's small population meant that issues and concerns in one realm influenced what happened in others. Metaphors were shared (as noted above, concerning economic efficiency and military battles), and the relationship between citizens and state was close enough that individuals could interact directly with the ruling elites through letters, petitions, or other texts, which were then preserved in the provincial archives. The impersonal aspects of state bureaucracy had not yet kicked into gear.

Third and most important, these decades were desperate times for most Albertans. Many of us are accustomed to thinking of the 1910s and 1920s as a golden age of progress and modernization, but in fact, for most rural Albertans, those years were a time of lurching from one crisis to the next, after a period of economic expansion.

Alberta became a province in 1905, with increased powers of self-government. The first decade of its existence was a time of giddy optimism and euphoric expansion for white settlers in Alberta, described as a "seemingly endless springtime" in Cavanaugh, Weatherell, and Payne's authoritative history of the province (Cavanaugh et al. 2006). Immigrants, mainly European, poured into the territory, so that its population increased more than fivefold between 1901 and 1911, from 73,002 to 374,295 (ibid., 382). The Aboriginal population was overwhelmed by the white arrivals, dropping from 20 per cent of the total population to only 3 per cent in ten years (ibid.). This boom was fuelled largely by a rush for cheap farmland now that the US Midwest was completely settled, as well as by historically high wheat prices, the expansion of the railways, and a federal government in Ottawa that wanted to settle Canada's empty spaces.

The dimensions of the boom can be gauged by indicators such as the number of real estate offices – there were four hundred each in Edmonton and Calgary – and the proliferation of rural towns, one after another, whose names are preserved today in the archival traces of their local newspapers (ibid., 364). The Hudson's Bay Company and the CPR sold off the land that had been given to them by federal law. Low mortgages, improvements in dryland farming, and the high demand for Canadian products such as grain, coal, and timber brought prosperity to the prairies. The number of grain elevators increased from 43 in 1906 to 279 in 1912 as the railway spurred the growth of small farms (Van Herk 2010, 182).

Plans to expand Edmonton and Calgary testify to the euphoria of those days. In large and small population centres, parades and other festivities celebrated the founding of "100,000 clubs" (or "50,000" or "25,000" clubs), whose purpose was to promote urban growth. Civic plans for Calgary alluded to Venice and Paris, and to boulevards, fountains, and public gardens (Van Herk 2010, 182). Meanwhile, money flooding into the towns from the countryside generated new spaces such as saloons and dance halls, along with soaring demand for cigarettes, alcohol, and luxury goods. At a time when a railway worker earned about $75 per month, hotels could, and did, charge up to 15 cents for a glass of beer. And all the while there was a constant flow of migrants from central Canada, the United States, Britain, and eastern Europe, drawn by relentlessly upbeat advertising about the fortunes to be made in Alberta.

This, the time of the Last Best West, marks the beginning of the historical period covered by this book. The first decade of the twentieth century was a golden age in Alberta, compared to the years between the two world wars, which Albertans experienced as a time of stress, disillusionment, and disappointment.

The hard times for Alberta began in 1913 with the bursting of the real estate bubble. The land rush had driven prices higher and higher until demand collapsed. Concurrently with this fall in demand, those who had purchased land found themselves increasingly unable to develop it, because they had spent all their money on the land itself, leaving no funds to develop it with. Also, many who purchased land found that they had been conned, learning too late that the lots they had bought either were swampland or were far too dry to produce the two crops per year they had been promised. The truly valuable land had been sold long ago, and many purchasers in urban and rural areas found themselves with unproductive, unsustainable assets. The construction of new towns and settlements ground to a halt, land offices closed, and bankruptcies increased. The men and women who had come to Alberta in the boom years now congregated in towns and cities; the result was a large and unstable mass of people without prospects. This alarmed the early Social Gospel proponents, such as those who founded the Beulah Home for girls and women who had "fallen prey" to idle young men.

The real estate collapse of 1913 was followed quickly by the First World War. At first, the war seemed to offer some economic respite through higher prices for wheat; however, this was more than offset by the slowdown in local markets for wheat, by the disappearance of male labour as men joined the Canadian army, and by the diversion of the state's productive resources into war preparation. Then in 1916, the first in a series of droughts struck the province, leaving farmers with "dust, weed, and bad debts" (Cavanaugh et al. 2006, 394).

The war also led to xenophobia: foreigners, mainly central Europeans, were perceived to be unpatriotic and deceitful, an enemy within. At the same time, antipathy developed towards single men who had not joined the war effort, who were viewed as shirking their duties. Social change fermented during the war years, manifesting itself in causes such as temperance and woman suffrage, but also in mistrust and hostility towards those perceived as "undeserving." High wartime prices and economic dislocation led to a wave of social unrest, spurred by unemployment and the inability of households to sustain themselves. Chapters 5 and 6 provide more details about the war years and their aftermath, and how this shaped the imaginative economy of reproduction.

One out of every eight Albertans who went overseas to fight was killed, and those who did return were often disturbed in body or mind. The war was followed immediately by the Spanish flu pandemic, which in 1918 struck 38,000 Albertans and killed at least 3,200, further decimating Alberta's economy (Cavanaugh et al., 2006, 421). And the flu was followed by a series of environmental crises, one after another, including droughts and floods, which afflicted Alberta several years before the Dust Bowl conditions of the American West made famous by John Steinbeck in *The Grapes of Wrath*. Especially hard hit was the Palliser Triangle, an arid region in the province's southeast, comprising roughly one-third of Alberta's agricultural land. Small towns that had come into existence only a few years earlier now disappeared from the map as farmers struggled to grow crops, failed, and abandoned their farms. The area depopulated rapidly, turning into rangeland for cattle. Foreclosures forced families out of rural areas and into cities, where there was little work and even less in the way of social welfare. Mortgage foreclosures in Edmonton and Calgary alone surpassed $28 million between the end of the war and 1922, and in the rural areas, 10,767 farms were taken by the state for unpaid taxes (ibid., 381). The ruling Liberal Party was ousted in favour of the populist United Farmers of Alberta (UFA), who promised to take the interests of small farmers to heart.

These desperate economic conditions blew families apart, as men abandoned wives and children either to seek sustenance elsewhere or to avoid responsibilities. A vigorous social welfare movement arose in 1920s Alberta, a bit later than in the rest of Canada, in response to rising poverty; it encompassed both the push for eugenic sterilization laws and pressure to provide allowances to abandoned or deserted mothers. However, during the 1920s human misery seemed to increase faster than any efforts to reduce it could match. This sense of fighting an inexorable advance of wretchedness comes across clearly in the writings of those were trying to implement these transformations (see chapters 4 and 5) – much more clearly than the optimism often associated with the Progressive Era in other locales.

A mild economic upswing in the late 1920s was soon overtaken by the Great Depression of the 1930s. Alberta was entirely dependent on exports – grain, lumber, coal – which were no longer economical to ship to distant markets, where demand had fallen. Poverty increased, as did the need for support to desperate families. In 1933, 27 per cent of Lethbridge's schoolchildren were classified as underweight (Cavanaugh et al. 2006, 493). Alberta voters tossed out the UFA and brought in a socially conservative, evangelically inspired Social Credit government in 1935 to apply radical solutions to economic crises.

The gloom would not lift until after the Second World War and the discovery of oil. Alberta, like many other North American jurisdictions, embarked on an age of prosperity in the late 1940s. But that is outside the purview of this book.

In terms of reproduction, the desperate decades of the 1910s through the 1930s posed challenge after challenge. Poverty and misery affected the survival of mothers and newborn children, which led to calls to protect these vital and threatened resources (see chapters 2 and 6). The dislocating effects of slow economic collapse also meant that more and more women were reproducing outside the normative heterosexual dyad, thus becoming problems for the collective (see chapters 3 and 5). Hard times also manifested themselves in calls to do something about the reproductive "enemy within" – the wrongful or undesirable reproduction of women who were classed as "feeble-minded"[3] or otherwise undesirable (see chapter 4).

Reproduction was an individual problem for many women, but it was also a problem for the wealthy and powerful elites of Alberta. When we read about state power being exercised, these elites were the ones at the helm. The Alberta elite was overwhelmingly male, Protestant, white, and of British descent, although as the years went by, some men from other ethnic and religious backgrounds made their way into its ranks.

Alberta legend holds that this province was the realm of the "self-made man," who parlayed a few quarter-sections of land, a few head of cattle, or a chain of small shops into financial and political clout. Such a man contrasted with the more effete male elite of eastern Canada, who inherited their wealth and status. Most members of Alberta's elite were "self-made men" – one of the enduring themes in Alberta biographical narratives is the story of the young man who comes out west, tries his hand at farming, and within a few years commands agricultural wealth and political power. Indeed, the elites of Alberta do appear to have sprung from humbler, more genuinely populist roots, compared to their contemporaries elsewhere. Both the UFA and (later) Social Credit were the products of grassroots politicking by agrarians, who combined a view of western modernity and progress with scepticism about the way things were done back east.

These men governed the welfare functions of Alberta, with enormous implications for reproduction. They decided who should be prohibited from reproducing (via the Sexual Sterilization Act), who might be deserving of assistance such as the mothers' allowance (despite having reproduced outside the heterosexual normative order), and whether women would survive childbirth (via debates over whether the province would support maternity care for pregnant women). With the Social Gospel and child-saving movements of the 1910s and 1920s, men (and some women) who had professional qualifications in social work or medicine also became involved in these efforts, bringing a degree of expertise to decision-making.

Alberta politics may have been the realm of the self-made man, but the boundaries between the state and private capital were porous, so that wealthy farmers, ranchers, or merchants also served as members of the provincial legislature. These individuals governed through paternalism and patronage, at least when it came to reproduction. Perhaps because of the small size of the settler population, bureaucracy, rationalization, and efficiency did not characterize decision-making. Individual women or families in distress would appeal for assistance directly to their representatives (or sometimes indirectly, through a reputable businessman in the community or a respected organization such as a church), be it for maternity care, for the support of an unmarried mother, or for money that would allow a women and her children to survive. Such assistance might be offered or withheld on a case-by-case basis. This heavily personalized style of government undoubtedly led to injustices and inequity; it also left a rich documentary trail of pleadings, complaints, considerations, and refusals, all of which generated the individual stories that animate these pages.

Sources

This book is based on archival sources, drawn primarily from the Provincial Archives of Alberta, located in Edmonton, and the University of Alberta's Peel's Prairie Provinces collection, which includes newspapers and other media as well as less formal texts. I also used the archives of the Glenbow Museum in Calgary, where many personal papers and collections are kept. In addition, I worked in several smaller archives: the City of Edmonton Archives, the South Peace Regional Archives in Grande Prairie, the Galt Archives in Lethbridge, and the Esplanade Archives in Medicine Hat. I would like to acknowledge the assistance of the staff at all these archives. I would also like to acknowledge the work of Ellen Whiteman, Sharon Springer, Daena Crosby, and Randi Nixon, who uncovered material for me. I appreciate comments from Julie Rak, Liane McTavish, Liz Czach, Joanne Minaker, Bryan Hogeveen, and anonymous reviewers for the *Canadian Journal of Sociology* on earlier drafts of different chapters. I appreciated the enthusiasm and guidance of Doug Hildebrand at University of Toronto Press in the preparation of this book.

This project was financially supported by the Killam Fund at the University of Alberta and by the Standard Grants program of the Social Sciences and Humanities Research Council of Canada. I would also like to express my appreciation for the presence of Michel Figeat and Rosie Kaler-Thompson during the writing of this book: Michel for his keen enthusiasm for local history, and Rosie for being a constant reminder of the wonders of making new people.

2 The Little Immigrant Who Comes into Our Homes: The Material Conditions of Childbirth

Introduction

Throughout this book, I will be arguing that women-as-mothers bore great weight in the symbolic imaginary of twentieth-century Alberta. However, as Wendy Mitchinson succinctly put it in her study of childbirth in twentieth-century Canada, "before a woman could become a mother, she had to give birth" (2002, 3). This chapter therefore takes up the question of childbirth – the concrete, material conditions of biological reproduction – and examines how the circumstances in which women brought babies into being became a focus of contestation and claims-making.

In doing so, I will be departing from much of the existing literature on the history of childbirth in Canada. Unlike Cynthia Comacchio (1993) or Denyse Baillargeon (2009), I will not be focusing on the emergence of "modern" obstetrics or on expert knowledge about birth in Alberta. And unlike Mitchinson, I will not be focusing on the actual experiences of women in labour and delivery. Instead, consistent with my concern about the imaginative economy of reproduction, I will be focusing on how people talked about giving birth and on the political and symbolic valence accorded to the options available to Albertan women: whether their babies would be born at home or in a medical facility; whether they would be attended by a nurse, a neighbour, or no one at all; and perhaps most important, what level of risk they would be asked to assume as they produced new Albertans for the greater society.

These were political and cultural questions, as well as medical and pragmatic ones. The social imaginary of childbirth in twentieth-century Alberta was rich and complex, involving ideas about danger, morality, progress, duty, and the future. It was filled with normative statements, not only about what mothers themselves "ought" to do – which has been the focus of many other studies of childbirth – but also about what "ought" to be done for these women. The mothers were imagined as simultaneously heroic and endangered. The figure of the expectant Albertan mother, the risks she ran, and the responsibilities she bore, not only for herself but for her society as she made new people for Alberta, emerged as a powerful political symbol. Yet the emotional and symbolic valence of this figure was not sufficient to compel state interventions commensurate to the problems she faced, and I suggest that this was due to ambivalence among the political elite and the medical profession regarding the costs and the value of medically attended births.[1]

Giving Birth in Alberta

For much of the first half of the twentieth century, women in Alberta relied on births at home. Aboriginal women had sources of information about safe childbirth within their own communities, in the form of women who were broadly recognized as midwives and older female relatives who were able to guide younger women through births. This social organization of births does not appear to have been radically changed by colonialism, unlike many other social forms in Aboriginal communities. Despite attempts to draw those communities into the orbit of white medical care, through churches, religious organizations, and federal government services, childbirth among Aboriginal women was largely left alone, to be managed within strong family and community networks. This situation persisted until the 1950s, when concerns for "sickly" Native mothers and infants led to efforts to change their labouring and childbirth practices (Jasen 1997). From the accounts of European settler women who suffered through complex births without support, medical or social, it appears that Aboriginal women fared better.

As Burnett (2010) documents, European settler women sometimes relied on nearby Native midwives to assist them through difficult childbirths. Mary Lawrence, for example, an English immigrant to remote Fort Vermilion and the daughter-in-law of an obstetrician, was favourably impressed by the standing and squatting positions for birth used by the Aboriginal women in her area; she wrote, "I was so convinced by the logic of this method over that to which white women are enforced that I abided by it henceforth" (M. Lawrence, "Keewaitin," Glenbow Archives, M3841; see also Langford 1995, 286). The memoirs of early nurses in Alberta who observed births managed by Aboriginal midwives also attest to this (e.g., Stewart 1979). But as Langford (1995) makes clear in her study of childbirth among European women in Alberta, the long distances between homes in rural areas and the cultural and linguistic barriers separating white women from Aboriginal women meant that hands-on cooperation between Aboriginal midwives and pregnant white women was the exception rather than the rule.

So who did attend births? The dominant narrative in the written history of childbirth in North America is the power struggle between physicians on the one hand, and midwives and lay women on the other, for the right and the capacity to attend births. In the first half of the twentieth century, doctors were actively expanding their turf, claiming more and more realms of human activity as medical concerns. In Canada, Mitchinson argues, the ascendancy of physicians' prerogative to attend births was especially pronounced. For instance, in two rural counties in Ontario, between 80 and 90 per cent of births were attended by doctors by 1913, and in urban Winnipeg the proportion was even higher – midwives attended only 5 per cent of births (Mitchinson 2002, 72). Canadian doctors were confident in their ascendancy as the masters of childbirth. As one professor of obstetrics and gynecology put it in 1929,

> we have committed ourselves for generations to a policy of physician-accoucheurs [birth attendants]. We cannot turn back now, even if we should wish to. Our policy has been an evolution, slow and cumulative. The physician-accoucheur has come to stay ... Our public (except those recent imports from the Near East) are not favourably disposed to midwives, and the public have the say as to who may or may not attend them in labour. (97)

Nonetheless, midwives in Canada did not disappear, despite the efforts of many doctors to render them superfluous. Contestations between doctors and midwives continued into the mid-century.

In Alberta, conflict between doctors and midwives was less pronounced than elsewhere in Canada. Alberta doctors did not compete actively against midwives for the prerogative of attending births, simply because there were not enough potential birth attendants, whether doctors or not, to meet the demand, especially in rural areas. Doctors, when they could be enticed to rural Alberta, tended not to stay long. Midwives were scarce in the white settler community because that community was demographically young, lacking the older generation of women who typically worked as lay midwives in the rest of Canada.

Aboriginal communities had strong midwifery traditions, but as noted earlier, white women did not usually avail themselves of these.

The dominant theme, then, in the history of births in Alberta is not the struggle for control over the birthing mother, but the dearth of parties to contest that struggle. Alberta physicians made sure the province's laws recognized them as the dominant authority over childbirth, even to the extent of trying to prevent midwives from gaining legal recognition (see below in this chapter). However, they showed little interest in putting that legal prerogative into practice, leaving a gap in skilled birth attendance for Alberta women. Thus the central political drama over childbirth did not revolve around competition between doctors and other birth attendants; rather, it took the form of contestation over whether women were entitled to any birth attendance at all.

In the early years, women gave birth at home, sometimes with the assistance of female relatives or neighbours, and sometimes entirely alone. Husbands and other men were involved in a minority of births; more commonly, men either retreated from the physical practices of birth or left the home to seek help while their wives were in labour. Early settlers who had immigrated from eastern Canada or Europe were also often cut off from sources of knowledge within their own social networks. As Langford writes,

> most women faced the limitations of their own ignorance of the birth pro-
> cess, but also of appropriate prenatal and postnatal care. These women
> were cut off from the usual support persons who surrounded women
> through pregnancy and childbirth. They had no regular access to the care
> and knowledge of mothers, sisters or aunts or even of friends and neigh-
> bours, except through letters. (1995, 280)

This theme – lack of knowledge about birth – was also taken up by the female writers for the *Grain Growers' Guide* and other populist periodicals, who called for what we would now refer to as comprehensive sex education so that women were not terrified by what awaited them when they gave birth.[2] The *Guide* offered farm women easy-to-read mail-order booklets with titles such as "How To Teach Children the Truth," "The Miracle of Life," and "Maternity Complete." These provided some factual information about how babies come into the world.

Whether or not women were well-informed about what lay ahead of them, they sought ways to deliver that minimized the dangers, which meant trying to avoid the possibility of giving birth alone in a remote farmhouse. In the 1910s and 1920s, a patchwork of private, small-scale institutions sprang up to meet the needs of women giving birth. Hospitals in the major cities began opening maternity wards in the early 1910s, beginning with the University of Alberta in 1911. Going to a hospital to give birth was expensive, however – the University of Alberta hospital charged $25 for a stay of up to twelve days (Vant and Cashman 1986, 125).

The main institutional form for women giving birth outside their own home was the small "maternity home." These were residential lodgings run by local women in small towns who styled themselves "matrons" or "sisters." Some of these women had formal nursing training; others did not. As Silverman (1998, 92) notes, these homes were, for women, one of the few means of earning income, especially in rural areas. The homes offered room and board to pregnant women, who would arrive at the maternity home up to a month in advance of their due date. The calculation of due dates was often imprecise, so women who did not want to be caught going into labour at home, especially during the winter, would come to the maternity home well in advance. The women who ran the home usually had formal or informal arrangements with local doctors, who would attend the births for a fee. These homes advertised in local newspapers, such as the *Red Deer News*: "Maternity nursing: Mrs. C W Wright will receive patients at her residence, 204 2nd Avenue North, where the best of care can be guaranteed at all times" (29 October 1929, 4); or the *Chinook Advance*: "Chinook Maternity Home. Cases Taken. $18 per week. Apply to Matron, Mrs. A Morin" (1 March 1917, 4).

As the number of maternity homes increased, they drew the attention of provincial politicians and subsequently fell under the authority of provincial regulators, who attempted to reserve childbirth to licensed medical practitioners. The first legislation regulating maternity homes, passed in 1918, required operators to obtain a licence from the local Board of Health, which could limit the number of clients and could charge the operator a registration fee. This legislation also required that every birth "be attended by a registered medical practitioner ... There must be at least one graduate nurse if the matron is not herself a nurse" ("New regulations for maternity homes through province," *Edmonton Bulletin*, 28 April 1921). However, the proliferation of advertisements in small-town newspapers for small-scale maternity homes, often operating out of the owner's home, suggests that attempts to regulate the homes did not impede their growth.[3]

Many of these women and their nursing homes became fixtures of rural communities, often receiving special mention in local histories. For instance, in *Taber Yesterday and Today*, a privately published 1951 compendium of "notable figures" in the history of that community, alongside the accounts about merchants and large-scale farmers, is one about "Mrs. Johnson," who "worked for many years on maternity cases of many kinds … She helped bring many of our earliest families into the world, one of special interest being Mrs. W V and all of her eight children" (66). Mrs Johnson was acknowledged as a community builder on par with political and economic leaders for her work in bringing new life into Taber.

Johanna Hakstad of Sexsmith, near Grande Prairie, is a striking example of a woman who became a recognized public figure in the 1920s and 1930s for providing childbirth care. According to the privately published history of the Sexsmith Women's Institute, which supported her work, Hakstad was indelibly shocked when a local sixteen-year-old girl gave birth to twins unassisted. (Hakstad herself had given birth to a daughter out of wedlock at the age of nineteen, with, it is suggested, very little support from her family or the community.) She learned the rudiments of midwifery by accompanying a local doctor but never trained formally as a nurse or midwife. She initially travelled to the homes of women in labour, where she would not only deliver the babies but also remain for up to ten days assisting with household chores. In 1929, Hakstad established the Sexsmith Maternity Home, also known as the "Stork Hospital," again in partnership with a local doctor, who would consult on complex cases.

By all accounts, Hakstad was a skilled practitioner who could handle complex or very premature births. She also did not require proof of marriage, which differentiated the "Stork Hospital" from other maternity homes. For all Hakstad's skills, maternal mortality was high – one eighteen-year-old woman died giving birth to a two-pound baby, eleven weeks prematurely. The baby was breastfed by the other mothers in the home at the time. Because Hakstad was not a trained nurse, she received no government grants or support for her work. The Sexsmith Women's Institute provided money to cover the costs of indigent women at her maternity home; it also brokered an introduction for Hakstad to Princess Alice of England, who was visiting northern Alberta on a morale-building tour during the Second World War. In 1948 an Appreciation Day was organized through the Women's Institute, and more than two thousand mothers from across the Peace River country contributed a dollar for each child born under her care, to be put towards a scholarship for nursing students to study obstetrics. Hakstad herself finally retired in 1958 (see South Peace Regional Archives, "Sexsmith Women's Institute 1934–1959," in *A Story of the Alberta Women's Institutes 1910–1937*, published by the Alberta Women's Institutes 1937).

For most Alberta women, however, the ideal childbirth did not take place at home with a midwife's help, or in a maternity home, but with attendance by clinically trained medical staff. This ideal was out of reach for a variety of reasons. Doctors were sporadically available from the earliest days of the twentieth century, but the quality of their care was variable, the turnover in rural areas was high, and the costs were exorbitant – in some cases upwards of $25 for simply being present at a birth (Langford 1995). Nurses or midwives might have provided cheaper services, but in the early years of the province, those who did attempt to provide childbirth services risked running afoul of the law and raising the ire of local doctors. It was commonly rumoured in rural districts that nurses could be jailed if they attended childbirth, especially if they also charged fees. Women in communities that were fortunate enough to have a trained nurse nearby – often the wife of a recent British immigrant – were often unsure as to whether they could legally engage her to help. In 1912, a group of women from a rural district wrote to the *Grain Growers' Guide*'s women's page:

> We have at last succeeded in getting a certified maternity nurse whom we consider a Godsend. She has been very busy already, and now the doctor tells us she is liable to a heavy fine if she practices down here. We are forty miles from the nearest doctor and fourteen miles from the one who speaks nothing but French. If the law in Canada is such, it is time your paper took up the question and agitated until it is changed. The nurse I am speaking about graduated from Queen Charlotte's Hospital [in London], and came out specially to our district. Kindly let me know if she is liable to prosecution as soon as possible. ("The Country Homemaker," *Grain Growers' Guide*, 11 December 1912, 10)

The editor of the women's pages, Francis Marion Beynon, responded that "there is no law preventing a nurse from practicing if she did not also practice medicine" (ibid.). Nonetheless, the precise conditions under which nurses could attend childbirth in a professional capacity remained opaque until the creation of the Department of Public Health and the District Nursing Service in 1919 (see below).

Prior to the creation of the Nursing Service, rural women who wanted a doctor to attend childbirth made individual arrangements with doctors, without a standardized fee schedule. The disparities in fees and the inaccessibility of doctors to women who had not managed to put a little money aside – a concern especially for farm women who experienced volatile producer prices for their harvests, or whose husbands controlled the proceeds from farming – preoccupied meetings of the United Farm Women of Alberta and other women's groups.

For instance, in 1914, the Stettler branch of the UFWA unanimously passed a resolution stating "that it is the opinion of this meeting that the inadequacy of medical attention in the rural districts is deplorable ... The number of deaths at maternity – largely preventable – is tragic" (*Grain Grower's Guide*, 5 August 1914, 8). The same month, the Hillview Women Grain Growers' Association devoted their meeting to health questions – in particular, the high cost and inaccessibility of childbirth services:

> After the usual business was disposed of, the topic "Doctor's fees on the Prairie" was led by Mrs. FA Boutz, who gave an excellent paper. An animated discussion followed. The chief points emphasized were that while doctors' fees on the prairie were necessarily high, yet particularly in maternity cases, prairie women should be provided with medical care at less cost. It was pointed out that while better farming trains are travelling for educational purposes and drill halls are being erected to prepare for possibilities which might never occur, something might be done to prevent the prairie baby from arriving with a chattel mortgage instead of the proverbial silver spoon in its mouth. ("Farm Women's Clubs," *Grain Growers' Guide*, 26 August 1914, 12)

"The Valley of the Shadow": Dangers of Childbirth

For most women in Alberta, the most salient fact about childbirth was that it was dangerous, frightening, and life-threatening. This risk lent a powerful symbolic and emotional valence to the figure of the expectant mother, poised on the threshold between death and new life. Wendy Mitchinson's authoritative history of childbirth in Canada suggests that expert medical opinion of the time was divided as to whether childbirth was intrinsically dangerous, or whether only certain births were problematic. However, the personal accounts of Alberta women themselves are permeated with awareness that during childbirth, death was close at hand. Nanci Langford's compilation of childbirth stories from early Alberta describes a time when "women literally risked their lives to establish their families and a future for their children." She succinctly summarizes the dangers facing women:

> The isolation, the poor trails and slow means of transportation, the uncomfortably hot or cold shack, the unpredictable weather, the lack of medical facilities and personnel, the lack of friends and relatives, the lack of compassion and understanding from her partner, her lack of knowledge about childbirth, her own weakened condition from overwork and an inadequate diet, and her inability to abandon even temporarily her responsibilities on the homestead. (1995, 279)

Langford's sources described the preparations women and their neighbours made before childbirth, on the assumption that they risked death. Sophie Puckette, in 1905, wrote of a neighbour expecting a child:

> She took me upstairs and showed me all her wedding outfit she had laid away carefully for them to put on her should she die. She imagines so strongly that her life will be given for the little life she is expecting in January that she has all her things put in order ... It made me want to cry to see the things all ready for her to die and to hear her talk of them. (cited in Langford 1995, 281)

Another early white settler, Peggy Holmes, wrote of her experience around the First World War:

> There were so many bereavements in the district. Two widowers were left with seven children each. That made fourteen more motherless children to be cared for. (ibid., 282)

In diaries and journals, childbirth was often conflated with death; women wrote of "going down into the valley of the shadow" as they prepared for birth.

Collectively, Alberta women expressed their fears of childbirth at venues such as the UFWA and the Women's Institutes, where the danger of maternal death often arose as a topic for discussion. For example, the Stettler branch of the UFWA in 1914 unanimously passed a resolution declaring that "it is the opinion of this meeting that the inadequacy of medical attention in the rural districts is deplorable ... and the number of deaths at maternity, largely preventable, is deplorable to say the least" (*Grain Growers' Guide*, 5 August 1914, 8). The annual conventions of the UFWA brought speaker after speaker and resolution after resolution concerning maternal health.

Perhaps inevitably, discussions of childbirth and the "valley of the shadow" were coloured by the metaphors of war. In 1916 the Canadian activist Violet McNaughton addressed the Homemakers' Convention on maternal mortality, imagining how a Canadian prisoner of war in Germany might explain his country to his captors. Such a prisoner would not be able to claim that Canada was a truly civilized society, said McNaughton, because "for so young a country, our roads and public buildings are truly remarkable, but on the prairies we leave our mothers to die of childbirth" ("Mothers left to die," *Grain Growers' Guide*, 12 July 1916, 10). Fifteen years later, in 1930, the UFWA unanimously passed a resolution calling for more medical support for mothers, on the grounds that "mothers' lives are far too precious to experiment with" (Minute Books of the UFWA Convention, 55, Glenbow Archives, M1749.44).

Medical workers shared the belief that childbirth was dangerous. Mary Percy Jackson, one of the first female doctors in Alberta, recalled decades later that "in Alberta having a baby, even in a city, was dangerous. The maternal mortality rate was 200 times as high as it is now ... So many women were out of reach of a doctor" (address to Professional Women's Club of Grande Prairie, 18 September 1985, Mary Percy Jackson fonds, Glenbow Archives, PR 1997.339).

Newspaper articles and speeches described childbirth as deadly and mothers as brave for risking death to bring new children into the world. These accounts were seasoned with outrage at this state of affairs. Marion Cran, a British journalist who toured western Canada investigating the conditions for prospective settlers, saw maternal mortality as the greatest problem faced by women on the prairies. In 1910 she described childbirth as "a hardship to be faced which makes women justly shrink from the country. First from one prairie wife, then from another, I heard a cry about the hardships of birth on the homesteads ... stories of courage, stories of disaster" (cited in Langford 1995, 282).

Was childbirth really so deadly? At the beginning of the twentieth century, no hard information was available about the dangers of childbirth in Canada. When such information began to be collected in the early 1920s, it confirmed what many prairie women intuitively felt: Alberta was a dangerous place to give birth. The 1920s were also a time of activism and agitation for women's health across Canada, with the conditions of reproduction at the forefront, as women's groups agitated for better gynecological and reproductive care, often tussling with doctors' associations over how that care should be provided (Mitchinson 2002; Comacchio 1993).

Helen MacMurchy, an Ontario woman doctor, wrote the first comprehensive report on maternal mortality in Canada in 1924. In this detailed statistical compendium, she singled out the west of Canada as particularly dangerous, noting that Alberta had the highest rate of maternal death in country, with 6.9 women dying for every thousand births (MacMurchy 1925, 194). She contended that the minimally acceptable rate of maternal death was two per thousand – in other words, that nearly 70 per cent of all maternal deaths were unnecessary and could have been prevented through medical care:

> Perhaps the day will come when people will look back and wonder why mothers have been held so cheap. It seems to me that the present day could solve the problems in such a way that no woman would have to take the risks of twenty years ago ... [but] this is the normal state of affairs in western Canada. (1924, 43)

MacMurchy's conclusions were picked up by the Alberta press, which reported on the state of maternal mortality as a scandal and a blot on the name of the new province. The *Edmonton Bulletin* informed readers that "for maternal mortality in childbirth, the records show that Alberta is the worst, with 6.7 [deaths] for every thousand births ... while the average for Canada is given as 4.7" ("Alberta's standing childbirth figures," 19 April 1923, 10).

Explanations for the dangers of childbirth varied. Medical experts like MacMurchy tended to blame ignorant mothers, unskilled midwives, and unhygienic practices, while women themselves attributed the dangers to isolation and lack of medical attention. Nonetheless, by the 1920s the dangers of childbirth had been established as a political and social problem for Alberta that demanded a political response in the name of fairness to women and for the sake of building up the province.

Safe Childbirth as a Political Demand

This equating of childbirth with risk of death heightened the political pressure to improve Alberta's skeletal health system. The need for safer

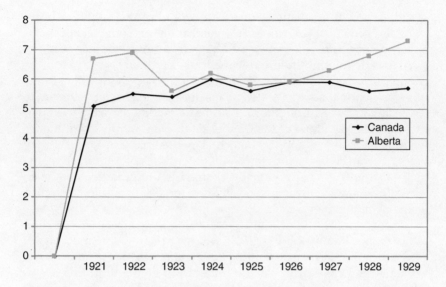

2.1 Maternal mortality in Canada and Alberta, maternal deaths per 1,000 births

Source: Corbett 1979, 93, from *Canada Year Book and Vital Statistics 1921–1929* [Ottawa: Queen's Printer].

childbirth (usually understood as childbirth under medical supervision) was framed as a political claim, something to which women were entitled as part of their work as nation-builders, bringing the next generation of Albertans into being. These claims emerged in the context of broader arguments about what was owed to the people settling Alberta – primarily white people of European descent – as part of the grand project of peopling the west. Many such claims emanated from newspapers, public meetings, and other sites of rhetoric as Albertans argued over the merits of different systems of political representation, the inequities of financial relationships with central Canadian banks and railways, the proper compensation for agriculture, and other topics during the ferment of the 1910s and 1920s.

Childbirth occupied a special status within these debates. It held both symbolic and practical importance: practically, safe childbirth was the best way to bring new people to Alberta; symbolically, it stood for the responsibilities of a society towards the people – mothers, in this case – who suffered and risked danger to build the society.

At the same time, disputes over who would provide childbirth services derailed efforts by women's organizations and others to press for better medical care for mothers. Doctors (most of them men) did not want to cede the right to provide medical care to any other group, including nurses or midwives, even though the supply of trained doctors was clearly inadequate. Politicians, for their part, were reluctant to create any form of subsidy for medical care that might result in higher taxes. The heroic figure of the frontier mother might rouse sentiments, but dollars-and-cents support for actual mothers came only after strong pressure from civil society. Here, as in other facets of reproduction, the mother served as an emotionally charged, morally laden icon, even while the haggling over responsibilities for flesh-and-blood women went on among men.

The concern for safe childbirth was primarily a concern about rural rather than urban women. By 1917, women in Edmonton and Calgary were much more likely than not to have some form of attendance by a doctor during childbirth, whether that meant giving birth in a hospital or having a doctor stop in at the home. According to the *Edmonton Bulletin*, in 1917, 1,461 births in Edmonton were attended by a physician, and only 129 were not. By contrast, for women living outside of the two main cities, physicians attended 5,400 births, while 4,202 had no physician in attendance ("Great provincial system of state-fostered public health in Alberta," *Edmonton Bulletin*, 28 March 1919, 1). This rate of physician attendance seems quite high and may reflect the non-registration of births that were attended by untrained midwives, family members, or no one at all.

The problem of childbirth was publicly identified with the condition of women living far from the main cities, on the edge of the frontier. The conditions of childbirth stood in for the sacrifices these women were making in order to populate the "wilderness" and spread Canadian civilization. The same editorial in the *Edmonton Bulletin* described the three things the state owed "the pioneer on the frontier settlement," – namely, "schools for the education of his children, highways to allow them to get to market and to make possible for him to receive medical attention and hospital care when needed" (ibid.). Within this list, childbirth was singled out as particularly deserving of attention: "The crying need today in the outlying districts is the absolute lack of medical and nursing attention and is sorely felt, particularly in maternity cases" (ibid.).

The *Grain Growers' Guide*, the voice of prairie populism, devoted several articles to the dangers faced by mothers, likening them once again to soldiers on the battlefield and demanding medical care for them:

> Why not apply to the creation of life as much attention as a lavished on the engines of death? The writer here repeats the demand for the establishment, in association with a system of maternity benefits, of a class of state obstetricians, competent and clean men and women, Listerian [that is, well-versed in theories of contagion] to their fingertips, who shall protect and serve the nation's mothers and keep them alive for future motherhood. This will certainly reduce infant mortality, it will save thousands of women from dying of negligence and carelessness, and it will leave half of our special hospitals for women untenanted since the crises of motherhood will no longer damage thousands of women for life. Surely the right of mothers today is that they shall not be poisoned or killed or damaged for life by our failure to apply the knowledge to this supreme cause, the creation of life that we already apply to its destruction on the battlefield. ("The culture of the racial life is the vital industry of any society." *Grain Growers' Guide*, 6 March 1912, 35)

Expanding on the military metaphor, the anonymous author defined pregnant women as efficient workers producing for society as a whole. Maternal care was needed not simply to protect individual women but to bolster a vital collective enterprise. "Our business is to recognize that the expectant mother is doing our work, and to take care of her accordingly" (ibid.). Stinting on prenatal or maternity care because of its cost was simply "sacrificing the future to the present" (ibid.).

The metaphors of efficiency and military victory dominated discussions of childbirth safety, just as they dominated talk about infant mortality, as I show in a later chapter. Mothers were viewed as essential workers in the task of peopling Alberta and were likened to soldiers who were wounded or killed in battle. Emmeline Pankhurst, the well-known British suffragist, made the connection explicit in her visit to Edmonton:

> "More women die in childbirth than men die on the battlefield" was the astounding statement made by Mrs. Pankhurst ... There was much talk of supplying 100,000 yearly immigration into Canada, but, said the speaker, vital statistics still showed that more than 20,000 babies died each year in Canada ... All classes of people are organized now for their own

protection, farmers, preachers, labourers, manufacturers, etc., but the greatest industry of all, the manufacture of the human race, was the only one not protected. Motherhood and marriage were the most risky of all occupations, said the speaker. ("Mrs. Pankhurst is speaker at big meeting last night held in the Memorial Hall," *Edmonton Bulletin*, 14 June 1923, 2)

Edward West, a British journalist whose *Homesteading: Two Prairie Seasons* purported to offer a frank account of the rewards and challenges of life in western Canada, condemned the Canadian government for neglecting childbirth. He similarly figured the mothers of Canada as victims on a battlefield:

> In the case of war involving what may be called a civilized nation, the people are aroused and great efforts are put forth to mitigate suffering, but it may well be questioned whether in the settling up of the prairie provinces, there has not been far more suffering entailed, especially on women and children, than a great war, and alas! It is still going on and will continue for many years unless a determined effort is put forth to stop it. (West 1918, 207)

While the First World War raged, Irene Parlby, the UFWA president, called for government support for childbirth:

> Is it not right that we should endeavour to adjust conditions [so] that every child born in the world shall have at least a fair chance of a healthy normal life; that every mother shall have the care that is her right, when she takes that journey into the valley of the shadow? (1917, cited in Ross-Kerr 1998, 91)

The national and provincial governments were indicted for their lack of care for frontier women undergoing childbirth. Both were viewed as irresponsible for not providing adequate services.

West harnessed the term "eugenics," with its connotations of science and progress,[4] to the cause of safer childbirth in Alberta:

> In all communities whose governments claim to be at all up to date, the care of mothers and children and what is called eugenics is receiving more and more attention, but the Canadian government, while receiving a splendid influx of life from the old countries, would seem to consider that

the gift of a hundred sixty acres of land [the standard land grant to new immigrants] covers a multitude of omissions in this respect. (1918, 206)

Similarly, Marion Cran, another enterprising British author (and a trained midwife), in her travel memoir *A Woman in Canada*, sharply accused Canada's governments, both federal and provincial, of neglecting childbirth. She described obstetric services as a "game of battledore and shuttlecock, the needs of women being the shuttlecock, between the greater and lesser governments" (Cran 1910, 96).

In taking up the call for medical attendance during childbirth, women's organizations and other populist outlets resorted to a number of rhetorical tropes and arguments. The most prominent such trope, not surprisingly, was the enlistment of obstetric services in the grand plan of "peopling" the prairies. In these arguments, the "peopling" was implicitly (and sometimes explicitly) understood to mean peopling by white Europeans. Filling up the prairies through natural increase – which would only happen when births were safe and reliable – was contrasted with filling up the West through immigration, the less desirable option.

Cran linked the dangers of childbirth to the unwillingness of British women to immigrate to Canada, or, once in Canada, to marry and move out to the rural areas of Alberta. She collected graphic accounts from rural women of the dangers they endured and their proximity to death, and linked all of this to the government's neglect of mothers:

[The farm woman's] life is straightforward, but it is greatly complicated when the babies begin to come … "Isn't he beautiful? But he was born before his time. You wouldn't think so, would you? I had to go so far to reach the hospital that the journey upset me and I was very afraid for him, he is nearly a month too soon … I am so glad to have him, but women suffer much out here in these wilds for lack of proper nurses. It is a dreadful thing to know how many prairie women go through their confinements alone. I was lucky I was able to get to a hospital, but lots of them can't." (ibid., 120)

I asked about the birth of her babies. Don't talk of it, she says. "I nearly died last time and thought poor Humpty must surely die. He was born hours before the doctor came and the nurse was on another case thirty miles off. I was alone but for Jim, he sent the chore boy for the doctor and he lost his way in the blizzard. Don't talk of it. We need nurses at reason-able distances all over the prairies – sensible, skilled women – but they are hard to get." The same cry as the first woman gave! If the Dominion gov-ernment would secure to itself a fine race it must watch the needs of moth-ers! (ibid., 136, emphasis added)

Cran's fellow Briton and Alberta-booster Edward West also conclud-ed that unsafe childbirth made for reluctant mothers, and reluctant im-migrants. He described the conditions in which rural women gave birth as similar to the battlefields of Europe, and he linked the conditions of childbirth to the reluctance of women to marry rural men:

It is true that a considerable number of women find employment in town who shrink from becoming wives and mothers on the prairie under pres-ent conditions, and without attempting to go into details or to elaborate the question, the thoughtful reader will perceive that such a state of things is not a healthy one for the future of the growing young nation.[5] (West 1918, 207–8)

Safe childbirth was also positioned as an alternative to immigration. In the *Wainwright Star*, an anonymous writer argued that mothers were as important as immigrants if not more so:

Canada's annual maternal death rate is something like four per day for each day of the year. For a population of less than 10,000,000 this is un-doubtedly a high average, especially when it is understood that Canadians congratulate themselves on being in the van[guard] of civilization ... Well intentioned people are saying that the government should come to the rescue. Quite properly it is urged that the conservation of the lives of our own people is at least as important as the attracting of new immigration. ("Maternity neglected is pitiable," *Wainwright Star*, 15 August 1928, 5)

Member of the Legislative Assembly went even further along this line of argument, claiming that safe childbirth was preferable to reliance on immigration for population growth. Babies, who would arrive in great-er numbers once the safety of their mothers had been secured, were described as new additions of high quality to Alberta's population, as compared to adult immigrants. In debates in the assembly over wheth-er user fees for childbirth services should be included in the legislation establishing municipal hospitals, MLA Louise McKinney pointed out that in New Zealand, new mothers received cash allowances to pay for the cost of having a doctor attend their births. That country, she said, "held that the best immigrants were those born into it" ("Hospital fees in rural plan rouses debate," *Edmonton Bulletin*, 19 March 1918, 1). The MLA from High River, Dr Stanley, was even more explicit about substituting safe childbirth for immigration. "The best immigrant is the little immigrant who comes into our homes," he declared, in a 1913 speech calling for "maternity grants for the wives of settlers" ("Bonuses for babies is remedy for infantile death rate," *Edmonton Bulletin*, 18 October 1913, 13).

Safer childbirth, then, would mean a better, stronger population for Canada, for women would be more willing to give birth if they believed they could do so safely, and babies would take the place of immigrants.

District Nursing and Childbirth

If childbirth was supremely deserving of resources and political support, and if safe motherhood was necessary to populate Alberta, why were no squadrons of doctors being dispatched to rural Alberta? Two obstacles stand out: the ambivalence of established health professions towards the work of assisting birth, and the cost of providing birth services.

During the early twentieth century, even while medical interventions such as "twilight sleep" and forceps use were being introduced into childbirth, Canadian doctors were divided among themselves as to whether birthing babies was beneath their dignity as professionals. Obstetrics was a low-status, low-prestige specialty, unless combined with gynecology, a surgical specialty that focused on pathological births (Mitchinson 2002). Outside the realm of doctors, even the Victorian Order of Nurses, which supplied public health nurses throughout much of Canada, attempted to hive off maternity nursing into a separate subcategory of nursing, less specialized than professional nursing, on the grounds that training as a nurse "made a woman too superior for maternity work" (Crain, cited in Relyea 1992, 16).

Nurses, who were struggling to establish themselves as true health professionals, may also have been put off by the forms of birth attendance practised by laywomen in parts of Canada and the United States, which often included spending days or weeks with the woman who had just delivered, assisting with household chores. Indeed, the National Council of Women, when it attempted to address the perceived lack of skilled birth attendants at the end of the nineteenth century, proposed a cadre of workers to be trained in obstetrics, who would be known as the Order of Home Helpers (Relyea 1992). This proposal met with indignant resistance from professional nurses, on the grounds that linking their work with "home help" would degrade the status of nurses. As a result of these professional concerns about the low prestige of attending births, health professionals were not queuing up to get access to pregnant and birthing women. Neither doctors nor nurses were clamouring for the opportunity to attend birthing women in Alberta.

Although professional infighting contributed to the lack of skilled birth attendants in early-twentieth-century Alberta, the more serious obstacle to better birth services was the question of how much it would cost. In the first two decades of the twentieth century, the almost entirely male Legislative Assembly repeatedly debated the pros and cons of providing financial support for childbirth, whether in the form of "maternity allowances" paid directly to women to cover the cost of doctors, or in the form of a universal health insurance scheme that would cover maternity. Despite constant reminders about the dangers of unattended childbirth and appeals on behalf of mothers who were risking their lives for their babies, MLAs repeatedly argued that the costs of either a maternity allowance or a comprehensive insurance system, whether paid out of provincial or municipal coffers, would lead to revolt by taxpayers.

The cost of childbirth was raised every time public health or health insurance came up for discussion. In 1918, MLAs voted down the Municipal Hospitals Act on the grounds that hospitals would be swamped by non-paying women in labour, and that the costs associated with this would discourage municipalities from opening hospitals at all ("Hospital fees in rural plan rouses debate," *Edmonton Bulletin*, 19 March 1918, 27). "Maternity cases" were specifically mentioned as a major contributor to Alberta's high death rates, but the use of public funds to subsidize the costs of childbirth, in order to save mothers and welcome the "little immigrants," was rejected repeatedly. Proposals for these services were rejected on the grounds that neither municipalities nor the province had an adequate tax base to support them. Maternal health was competing for government money with infectious diseases (especially tuberculosis and influenza) and with child health programs such as immunization. The labouring mother in the shadow of death might raise sympathies but could not raise money.

In 1919, however, advocates for maternal health found a way around the provincial aversion to paying for birth services. While the male politicians in the Legislative Assembly fretted about the cost of maternal health services, the province's women's organizations drove the issue forward, keeping safe childbirth front and centre in their political agitation. In the early 1910s, these groups agitated for the creation of a district nursing scheme in rural areas that would focus on maternity care. After the Albert District Nursing Service was inaugurated in 1919, these groups continued to press for more nurses to attend births and for some financial relief for mothers who were unable to pay for their services.

The moment was auspicious for the creation of the Nursing Service. The First World War had drawn public attention to the state of health of Albertans, as families and households faltered under the loss of male breadwinners and workers and as doctors' grip on medical work was loosened by the shortage of medical staff, who had been drawn away by the war. By then, other jurisdictions in the British Empire were establishing public health systems (e.g., travelling nurses), so Alberta was following the lead of other jurisdictions (however, in Canada only New Brunswick had established district nursing before Alberta).

The very existence in Alberta of a provincial public health department was the result of the intense demand for childbirth services, voiced by the same women who were advocating for suffrage and other women's rights – in particular, Irene Parlby and Violet McNaughton. Histories of medicine in Alberta make it clear that the primary function of that department, especially in its early days, was maternity care (Ross-Kerr 1998, 94–7).[6] The newly created department launched its District Nursing Service by sending two trained obstetric nurses out to the remote Peace River country; six more followed in 1921, and eight in 1934. By 1939 there were twenty-five such nurses, who made barely a dent in the demand for nursing services (Richardson 1995, 1–9).

Districts had to petition the provincial government for visiting nurses. They were not automatically assigned, and were supplied only if there was proof that no doctor was available in the district. Also, each district was responsible for providing accommodation and food for the nurses assigned to it, who would be too busy to grow their own – in any case, shopping for food was impossible in many districts. Mary Conlin Sterritt, one of the first two nurses, recalled that although district nurses were "qualified to accept full responsibility for all cases of illness, emergency and maternity cases, the latter [was] the most important part of their work" (ibid.). District nurses charged much less than doctors – usually around $10 per birth, which included pre- and post-natal services as well as attendance at the birth itself. When families were unable to pay cash, the local board of health might accept payment in kind, such as cords of firewood (Stewart 1979, 16). District nurse Philippa Chapman, who worked in Valleyview and Leduc, recalled that

> the District Nursing Service really started because of the maternity needs of the homesteaders' wives. No one had any money, and so they would seldom call a doctor. If they went to a hospital with no money, they would be put on relief and it became a charge against their lands [i.e. their farm could be forfeited to the district if they were unable to pay back their hospital bills]. (cited in Ross-Kerr 1998, 101)

Perhaps not surprisingly, the District Nursing Service had to be very careful to avoid professional turf wars with physicians, who, although their numbers were too small to meet the demand for obstetric services, nonetheless regarded medical care as their prerogative and resisted incursions by other caregivers. In the early years of the twentieth century, only doctors had the legal right to charge fees for attending births, according to an 1885 ordinance left over from the days when Alberta was part of the Northwest Territories. This placed the few women in Alberta who had midwifery training in an awkward legal position (Langford 1995, 285). The creation of the district nursing scheme represented a compromise between the territorial protectiveness of doctors and the need for skilled attendance at births. The Public Health Nurses Act of May 1917, which regulated this new group of practitioners, stated explicitly that nurses with training in obstetrics could attend births only when "in the opinion of the Minister the services of a registered medical practitioner are not available" (cited in Stewart 1979, 49). It was illegal for public health nurses with only general training to attend births under any circumstances; only those who had completed a special course in obstetrics could do so.

But this special training was unavailable in Alberta until 1934, when an obstetrics training centre was established in Alder Flats and a midwifery course was inaugurated at the University of Alberta. Before then, the majority of nurses with obstetrics training had received their education in midwifery in England. As a result, the few nurses who had specialized training in childbirth often found themselves devoting all their time to obstetrics. For instance, Mrs Barnes, the only nurse with specific obstetrics training based in Lethbridge in the 1920s, was often "dated up" with childbirth cases for months in advance, leaving her no time for holidays and no time to relieve any of the hospital-based

Lethbridge nurses (Ross-Kerr 1998, 26). The memoirs of district nurses of those days are filled with accounts of arduous travel, complex birth emergencies, and cultural perplexities as the overwhelmingly anglo nursing staff interacted with women of eastern European, Slavic, and Métis origins (Ross-Kerr 1998).

In 1930 the provincial government gradually began to increase the presence of physicians rather than nurses in rural areas, hiring doctors directly in four districts and subsidizing the costs of private physicians in eleven others (Langford 1995, 292). During the 1930s, the UFA government actively recruited British female doctors to come to Alberta, advertising for "strong energetic medical women" for whom "the ability to ride a saddle horse would be an advantage," according to Mary Percy Jackson, one such British recruit (Jackson address to Professional Women's Club of Grande Prairie, 18 September 1985, Mary Percy Jackson fonds, Glenbow Archives). Jackson was assigned to the territory of Battle River as the sole physician for more than four hundred square miles, whose primary responsibility would be overseeing births.

In 1944, Alberta enacted maternity hospitalization legislation, which accelerated the push towards hospitals as venues for childbirth. Expectant mothers who were "bona fide residents of the province" could receive up to thirteen days' living expenses for the mother and newborn baby, if they gave birth at one of ninety-six hospitals and forty nursing homes. These benefits, the first such in Canada, were expected to "relieve 18,000 families a year of approximately $50 each" ("Alberta leads dominion in free maternity cases," *Wainwright Star*, 5 April 1944, 1). By the end of the Second World War, doctor-attended births had become the norm in Alberta, although in rural areas the district nurses continued to attend a large portion of cases and maternity homes continued to operate into the 1950s.

Conclusion

In Alberta, childbirth as a social and political event was filled with paradoxes and contradictions. Unlike other parts of Canada, the struggle over birthing was not mainly a turf war between physicians and other attendants over who had a right to attend births; rather, it was largely a struggle to accord women any support in birthing at all. Physicians did try to keep other birth attendants out of the field, but these manoeuvres were secondary to the real drama regarding childbirth in Alberta – the need for help of any kind for pregnant women. On the western frontier, long distances and scarce medical staff, combined with the financial hardships of the 1910s and 1920s, produced a situation in which pregnant women were left largely to their own devices, or to the informal assistance of neighbours, if they were lucky. The small and scattered private maternity homes that sprang up to meet obstetric needs inspired loyalty from the women they served but were hemmed in by legislation that defined birth as the province of medical staff, even when there were no medical staff.

The paucity of safe birthing options gave rise to efforts by women's organizations and sympathetic politicians to define birth as a social and political crisis besides an individual one. The image of the endangered mother going down into the shadow of death for the sake of her children was a powerfully dramatic one, and it was deployed to make claims and stake out moral territory. These mothers were configured as part martyr and part soldier – they were risking their lives for the greater good, using their bodies as weapons in the battle for Alberta's future. In the rhetoric of those who advocated state-supported childbirth, the valour of the mothers was opposed to the apparent indifference of the state, which held women's lives cheaply even as it depended on the new lives that women brought forth.

By the end of the First World War, these efforts had paid off in the form of the District Nursing Service, Alberta's first venture into public health. This service was strategically organized around the need for birth services, premised on women's entitlement to safe passage through the valley of the shadow as they produced the next generation of Albertans.

3 Treasures: Multiple Economies of Reproduction at the Beulah Rescue Home

How about doing some part of your Christmas shopping in the basement of the Legislative building this year? What could make a grander Christmas present than a darling baby?

(clipping: "Baby adoption a Christmas gift idea," n.d., November 1938)

Introduction

From the conditions of birth in general, we move now in this chapter and the following one to consider particular births – the ones that were defined as politically or socially problematic in early Alberta. First we consider births identified as illegitimate – that is, as happening outside normative marriage.

The setting for this investigation is the Beulah Rescue Home for unmarried mothers. Its former location at the intersection of 137th Avenue and 99th Street in Edmonton, Alberta, is today a nondescript bit of inner-ring suburbia, dominated by an aging mall, rush hour traffic, and franchised "family restaurants." Yet for more than half of Edmonton's history, it was the physical and symbolic nexus for the management of illicit pregnancy. In this chapter, I examine Beulah as a site of multiple economies of reproduction, generated through the efforts of the Beulah staff and the wider society to contain, redeem, and transform unmarried pregnant women and their infants.

The first historians and sociologists to study the governance of pregnancies outside normative frameworks of marriage did so from a deviance/psychology perspective in which the pathologization of individual girls was at issue (e.g., Vincent 1960; Friedman 1975; Rains 1970;

for an overview, see Brush 1997; Spensky 1992; Solinger 2000). More recent work, strongly influenced by feminist and Foucauldian theory, has moved away from the question of individual deviance to focus on unmarried mothers as the subjects of governance, enmeshed in the bio-politics of their times (e.g. Reeves 1993; Murray 2004; Levesque 1994; Little 1998; Strange 1995). This body of work also draws from the influential idea of stratified reproduction developed by Shellee Colen (1990) and popularized through the widely cited work of Faye Ginsburg and Rayna Rapp (1995) on reproduction and social theory.

The idea that social value is generated through some pregnancies but not through others links stratified reproduction to the much broader field of the *political economy of reproduction* (Greenhalgh 1995; Greenhalgh and Li 1995; Browner 2000; McDaniel 1996; Riley 1999; Kaler 2000, 2004; Rapp 2001; Ginsburg and Rapp 1995). In this perspective, reproduction is imagined as a situationally contingent and socially directed process in which the accumulation, consumption, and distribution of resources are shaped by asymmetric power relations among individuals and collectives. In this chapter, I take political economy of reproduction as a point of departure. However, while most authors speak of *a* or *the* political economy of reproduction, I want to suggest that reproduction in any circumstances consists of *multiple* simultaneous economies, imaginary and material, that intersect, reinforce, and contradict one another.

By "economies," I mean observable patterns in the accumulation, distribution, conversion, and circulation of valued resources, whether those resources are concrete or symbolic.[1] To illustrate the idea of multiple simultaneous economies, I look at two distinct patterns of accumulation, distribution, and circulation of resources at work in twentieth-century Alberta, brought into existence through the work of the Beulah Rescue Home. These are what I call the *economy of feminine virtue*, by which I mean the attribution of goodness and innocence to individuals, which attribution is convertible into entitlement and claims on other forms of resources; and the *economy of babies*, focusing on the distribution of the adoptable infants born at Beulah.

The first economy is mainly symbolic; the second is as concrete and corporeal as it is possible to be. Yet these two economies intersect with each other and are mutually dependent. The interdependence of these economies is perhaps most obvious in the words used to describe them – both the feminine virtue of the "fallen" women who became pregnant and the babies themselves were frequently referred to as "treasures," "precious," and even "jewels." The subject of this chapter is the material and discursive work that was required in order to assign value to these entities both symbolic and corporeal, and to accumulate and distribute this value.

Beulah assisted women variously referred to as "unfortunate," "fallen," "in trouble," and "in a certain way" between 1909 and 1964. Beulah provided women who were pregnant with residential accommodation before, during, and after the birth of their child, along with medical services; it also made efforts to socially and morally rehabilitate the "disgraced" mothers, within a Christian ethos that emphasized compassion and forgiveness. The home was also the centre of distribution for the children born of these pregnancies, whether these children were taken by their biological mothers immediately after birth, boarded at Beulah until the biological mothers could secure accommodation and retrieve their children, placed for adoption with other families, or turned over to the custody of the provincial Department of Neglected Children, later the Department of Social Welfare.

This chapter draws on the records of the Beulah Home in the Provincial Archives of Alberta. These records consist largely of the vast personal papers of some of Beulah's longest-serving staffers, who maintained detailed scrapbooks,[2] ledgers, and correspondences. The continuity of these staffers – in particular Mary Finley, the superintendent from 1921 until 1964, long-serving nurse Olivia Eidsath, and board of directors leader Charles Hill – meant that many ideas and practices at Beulah remained consistent across its decades of existence, although the home was most active in the late 1910s through to the 1940s. Records containing details of individual clients, including their own accounts of their circumstances, are protected by Canada's privacy legislation and are not used in this chapter, which means that the voices of the clients themselves are necessarily obscured by institutional texts.

Beulah was a privately funded institution, which creates both constraints and opportunities for researchers. Because it was not state-funded, it was not subject to reporting requirements that would have systematically preserved quantifiable information about the operations of the home. It was also not part of the Salvation Army or the Catholic Church, which ran the largest chains of maternity homes in Canada and kept records of their member institutions. On the other hand, because Beulah had to constantly, persistently, and creatively appeal for donations and support, the Beulah staff and advocates created an enormous archive of texts representing Beulah and its mission to audiences both broad and narrow. They were assisted in this by enthusiastic support from the local press: the *Edmonton Bulletin* and later the *Edmonton Journal*.

An Overview of Beulah

Edmonton, the site of Beulah, has always been a frontier city, the gateway to Canada's vast northwest. Beulah Rescue Home opened in 1909 as an offshoot of the Beulah Rescue Mission, which had opened two years earlier to cater to the growing transient urban population during an economic boom. It was run by the Mennonite Brethren in Christ, although its literature describes it as "nondenominational." The mission focused at first on providing food, shelter, and a large dose of evangelism to indigent men. From its earliest days, though, the mission workers encountered women and girls in Edmonton's demi-monde – sex trade workers, alcoholic women, and women with unplanned, "illegal" pregnancies – whose needs were pressing. In 1909 the mission rented a house to shelter these women away from the men and named it the Beulah Rescue Home. The mission stayed open to cater for men; the new home (a word connoting domesticity) would be for women. The home moved twice in its first years of existence, as each location was found unsatisfactory because it was too close to the temptations of Edmonton's downtown.

In 1911 a new, purpose-built home was opened on what was then the outskirts of Edmonton at 99th Street and 137th Avenue, on agricultural land donated by a prominent businessman – an early sign of the close relationship between Beulah and Edmonton's elite. This relocation marked the true beginning of Beulah as a home for unmarried pregnant women, as distinct from an institution catering to women in all forms of distress. In effect, this separated the girls who might yet be redeemed from their "fall" into unmarried motherhood from those who were viewed as unregenerate participants in the demi-monde. The Beulah board of directors approved this move because it would enable them to keep the "girls who had been deceived" separate from "the women of the underworld" (i.e., sex trade workers) (Beulah Home Board of Directors minutes 1913, PAA[3] PR 1971.004, box 1). Beulah thus effected a literal spatial sorting of women into Madonnas and whores.

By its seventh anniversary in 1916, Beulah could claim to have "rescued" ninety girls in the preceding year, with seven girls and four babies in residence on the annual "open day,"[4] when the people of Edmonton were invited to tour the home. The annual intake of women grew steadily over the next four decades, peaking at about 170 intakes per year in the late 1950s, the last years for which this information is available. Throughout these decades, Beulah was run by its matron and superintendent Mary Finlay, a deeply religious woman who had begun working at Beulah in the 1910s, left briefly for a marriage ending in early widowhood, and returned as superintendent in 1922. She would retain that position until her retirement in 1964. In a retrospective newspaper article in 1958, she was described as "foster mother to 3,800 babies" who had been born at Beulah during her tenure. Mrs Finlay's staff consisted of a cadre of "baby nurses" and general assistants – many of them also very long-serving – as well as a group of Edmonton doctors who attended births in Edmonton hospitals and, later, when Beulah's own hospital wing was opened in 1927, at the home itself.

Beulah does not appear to have been run along the lines of other maternity homes in North America and Europe, when compared to the accounts provided by Levesque (1994), Petrie (1998), Solinger (2000), Murray (2004), Garrett (2000), Luddy (2011), Thane (2011), and others. In these accounts, such homes were sites for the routinized production of shame and correction, an infamous example being the Magdalen laundries in Ireland. Beulah was powered by a different Christian ethos, one that emphasized love, compassion, and forgiveness for those girls who were willing to accept being rescued. This acceptance entailed incorporation into a model "family" at the home. Beulah clients were encouraged to think of the staff as mothers and grandmothers, and their fellow clients as sisters, even though their residence with this "family" was a matter of weeks or months. In the matron's monthly report to the board of directors, when an account was given of how many women or infants joined the family or left it, the entire population of the home – clients, staff, and babies – were referred to as "the Beulah family." What the clients themselves thought of this familialization is not known, although Beulah's files contain many letters from former clients and staff claiming nostalgia and affection for the particular atmosphere of the home. In 1944, one girl wrote:

> I certainly miss everybody. Every time I get the blues there is only one place that I usually want to go to again. I'd often walk over in the evening only I'm so afraid I will run into someone I know. I always think of chapel Thursday night and Sunday school on Sunday and I really wish I could attend them again. Honestly I really miss all the things I enjoyed so, there with all of you. (PAA, Beulah Home fonds, PR0803, "Annual Report 1944")

This testimony was used in an annual report for fundraising purposes, which may make it suspect, but other handwritten letters, apparently sincere, suggest that Beulah was remembered fondly – or at least, was remembered as a better alternative than the others available to single women at the time, both clients and staff. One staff member, who had resigned to care for a sick mother as the only unmarried daughter, reminisced:

> Beulah, home for the staff, for the precious girls, and for the darling little babies ... oh how I want to come home, how I want to be part of that precious fellowship that you will be sharing, to be one in the bond that unites us closer than sisters. But duty calls and I must stay. (letter from "N Pratt," 9 September 1949, PAA PR0803).

While Finlay and other Beulah administrators encouraged, and received, great loyalty from staff, their most important relationships were with donors to the home. Beulah received no direct provincial funding. It had two main sources of revenue: first, the fees paid by the inhabitants themselves, to cover medical costs and the costs of boarding their baby; and second, donations from the public, for which the Beulah staff canvassed tirelessly. Donors to Beulah were a cross-section of Alberta philanthropy; they included small-town Women's Institutes, which contributed knitted blankets and socks; wealthy local women; church groups; municipal authorities from whose rural districts the Beulah clients came; the Edmonton Community Chest (later the United way); and newspaper readers, who were encouraged to sponsor a baby or a mother for as little as fifty-nine cents a day (pamphlet: "Did You Know [Facts About Beulah Home]," 1931, PAA PR0803). The Beulah staff also courted wealthy and influential women in Edmonton, often the wives of prominent businessmen, through regular "open days" and teas during which donors and guests could tour the grounds, admire the babies in residence, and hear stories from some of the young women.

Beulah's fundraising efforts were enthusiastically supported by the local press, which often ran features in which the tragedies of the clients' backgrounds were juxtaposed with the brief idyllic period of quasi-family life they found at Beulah. The local press, especially the *Edmonton Bulletin*, also cooperated in ventures such as the Christmas adopt-a-baby drive (of which more later) and the 1928 appeal for 5,000 one-dollar bills ("The babies are reaching out little hands to YOU now. Have you sent your dollar? Mail it NOW please" ["Babies needing help," date unclear but probably January 1928, PR0803]). Much of the imagination and energy of Beulah's staff went into crafting these appeals to different audiences, framing the women, the circumstances of their pregnancies, and their babies in such a way as to generate the greatest amount of compassion and donation possible.

The demographic make-up of Beulah clients is hard to ascertain. Finlay and the Beulah administration had an interest in representing their clients as young girls, barely out of childhood and still partaking in the innocence of childhood, which led them to be easy pickings for deceptive older men, as distinct from "hard cases," older women who had sex repeatedly outside marriage for money or for pleasure, and who were not welcomed at Beulah's rural idyll. Beulah's clients were almost always referred to as "girl-mothers" or "child-mothers," and the short biographical sketches that accompanied appeals for funds focused on barely adolescent girls, often bereft of mothers themselves. One particular story about a fourteen-year-old girl who found herself pregnant appeared repeatedly. However, other evidence suggests that Beulah's clients may not have been entirely or even predominantly children or "girl-mothers." Because the home was largely privately supported, it was not required to complete detailed annual reports on the composition of its clients, so figures are hard to come by. Nonetheless, a 1947 article on Mrs Finlay's long service reported that "mothers have come from various fields and occupations ... Included are waitresses, clerks and factory workers 36%; domestic workers 20%; girls living previously at home 19%; in professions 18%; school girls 6%" (PAA PR0803). Thirty years earlier, at Beulah's sixth-anniversary festivities, the matron Mrs White informed that audience that twenty-eight girls had been helped over the course of the year thus far, but in her breakdown of numbers, only five were listed as being under eighteen.

Beulah may have been located in a remote corner of Canada, but it was connected through networks of evangelism and missionary activity to a much broader geographic field. Beulah's staff were keenly aware that they were part of a worldwide endeavour to uplift and Christianize both those who had never encountered Christianity and those who, like the Beulah clients, had fallen away. Senior staff moved between Beulah and other rescue missions in Canada and the United States, and evangelists and proponents of mission work visited Beulah to observe its work. Finlay herself had strong links to overseas mission work, with relatives and in-laws in Nigeria. The 1946 anniversary address celebrated the dispersal of Beulah's babies, clients, and adoptive families across Colombia, Ecuador, China, India, and the West Indies, "as well as the home land." "So the ministry of Beulah reaches out, internationally as well as interdenominationally," concluded the address ("1946 anniversary," PAA PR 1971.004, box 1).

Beulah's clients came to the home through self-referral, through referral by doctors or by Edmonton's Social Welfare Department, and, especially in the early years, through the Police Department. Fees were charged, beginning at $130 for a three-month stay. This included the doctor's fee for delivery, a charge that "shall be made in all instances against the father of the child where he is found" (PAA 93.359, Beulah Home minutes, minutes for 27 March 1925). In many cases, the municipal welfare department paid the charges; in an unknown number of other cases, the client could "work off" her fees after the child's birth by doing work around the home, including caring for the babies in the nursery. The average length of stay appears to have been around three months.

Once the babies were born, clients had the option of keeping the baby with them, or placing the baby for adoption by making the infant a ward of the state. In the literature on maternity homes, the question of just how much freedom the clients had in making decisions about their children's future is prominent. There are many accounts of women being coaxed, coerced, or deceived into agreeing to have their child adopted. At Beulah, the subtle pressures that may have been exerted on clients to place babies for adoption are lost to history. However, the written record suggests that the Beulah administration was openly supportive of clients keeping their babies, even in the earliest years, when the stigma of unmarried motherhood was strongest. The increasing number of "girls making good and keeping their babies" was described as "an encouraging result" for 1923, and the 1925 Annual Report noted approvingly that "there is a growing sympathy for the mother who keeps her child and we trust that this will continue to increase" (29 January 1924 minutes; see also "1925 Annual Report," PAA 93.359, Beulah Home minutes).

Beulah clients who chose not to place their child for adoption but who were unable to set up a living situation that could accommodate a baby were able to board their babies at Beulah until they were able to reclaim them. In theory, babies could be boarded for a year; in practice, some were boarded well into toddlerhood. The cost of boarding a baby in the 1930s was $5 per month. The expansion of Beulah's nursery facilities, so that more women would be able to board their babies instead of placing them for adoption, was the theme of a 1924 fundraising campaign. Interviewed for a newspaper article promoting the expansion, Finlay said that "as time goes on, more and more of the girls are planning to keep their babies. None of them wanted to give them up, but sometimes they are driven to do so because they can see no way to keep them ... Every girl wants to." ("Expansion for baby home," n.d., probably 1924, PAA PR0803).

Beulah's 1929 Christmas letter to donors stated that 50 per cent of the babies were kept by their mothers and that the other 50 per cent were available for adoption. This ratio appears to have fluctuated between one-half and one-third throughout the decades and appears quite different from the average for Canadian maternity homes, in which in the 1950s around 80 per cent of babies were placed for adoption (Petrie 1988).

If Beulah looked favourably on mothers keeping their children, other Edmonton institutions did not. As late as the 1950s, the Beulah Board of Directors expressed concern about other bureaucrats, especially in the provincial child welfare department, pressuring mothers to place their children for adoption. Part of this pressure apparently involved telling unmarried pregnant women to give birth at the city hospital, where it was easier to separate mother and baby, rather than at Beulah:

> [The superintendent of the child welfare department] seems quite convinced that it is better to persuade every mother to give up her baby. They can go to a local hospital and if they wish never see their baby and leave as soon as able. [The deputy superintendent,] I believe, is also urging this measure – for the sake of the baby, they say ... We are anxious to help rebuild character in the girl and also give the baby a reasonable start in life. ("Superintendent's Report to Board of Directors 1955," PAA 93.359, Beulah Home minutes)

By the 1950s, Beulah's work was slowing down. The number of clients per year peaked in 1955 at 171 and then began to decline. By 1961, "there is a tolerance in the public mind today that was unknown a few years ago, hence the majority of the unwed mothers move about in public without embarrassment" ("Board of Directors – 1961 Superintendent's Report," PAA 93.359, Beulah Home minutes). Hospital facilities had become more accessible and more accommodating to unmarried women, and fewer sought out the discretion of Beulah. Also, reforms to social welfare regulations had made it more feasible for single mothers to raise their children, so the role of Beulah in brokering adoptions was no longer as necessary. In 1963 the nursery at Beulah was closed and all infants were moved to a central city facility. In 1979, following the liberalization of laws governing contraception and abortion, the home itself was closed, and in 1983 the Beulah Rescue Home was officially dissolved. The Mary A. Finlay Manor for senior citizens took its place nearby.

An Economy of Virtue

As Nurse Pratt's letter makes clear, Beulah was fuelled by affect and a sense of morality. In this it was similar to other maternity homes in which emotion – especially "feminized" emotions of pity, compassion, and affection – drove (or were accused of driving) the work of the home. Kunzel (1995) quotes critics of American maternity homes complaining about the "superheated emotional atmosphere of pseudo-moral indignation" in the homes, and the "maudlin sentimentality" with which the staff regarded the clients and one another (quoted at 26; see also Murray 2004). Kunzel disagrees with this harsh assessment, pointing out that in the gendered division of charity work in the early twentieth century, "emotion, intuition, empathy and piety ... were the tools of the trade of womanly benevolence" (24). At Beulah, these emotional expressions centred on the figure of the young "child-mother" divested of her most precious currency, her sexual purity, and animated the institutional effort of raising the value of that currency again.

Affect and morality thus blended in what I call the "economy of virtue" at Beulah, an economy in which clients, staff, and even adoptive parents partook. I am using the term "virtue" in the same narrow sense as it is used in the Beulah archives, to refer to an intrinsic gendered value or worth, located in but distinct from the self, grounded in sexual history but not reducible to it. For the clients of Beulah, their virtue was imagined as a precious form of capital that they had either lost or been cheated of through fraudulent transactions, but that could be replenished through the investment of time, emotion, sacrifice, and spiritual grace. Clients were never considered "ruined" at Beulah – instead, they were perceived as being at a low point in their fortunes, but redeemable.

How did these women lose their virtue? The Beulah archive presents one hegemonic narrative: a young virgin, always referred to as a "girl" and usually described as being without family protection, is tricked into sexual activity with predatory men and, to her own surprise and terror, becomes pregnant. A Moravian minister associated with Beulah opined that "some of these poor girls get an awful shock when they find out what bitter tears the results of sin can bring" ("Twenty-Five Years of Rescue Work at Beulah Home," 27, PR0803). Edmonton is figured as a city of vice in which a "transient class" of men flourished, creating temptations for a girl to "spend" her treasured virginity in the same bars and hotels where men spent their wages. A typically melodramatic example of this narrative of loss and expenditure was probably written by the first matron of Beulah, Elizabeth Chatham:

> We have scores of young women from the old country [Great Britain]. The wages paid for domestic service here are much better than at home and they expect to help their people by their earnings, but alas! Their plans and good intentions are spoiled for the trap has been laid! They are left broken hearted, robbed of their virtue, with the prospect of becoming a mother and facing the world in disgrace. You ask why? Well, she comes here unprotected, a great many of them with not even a relative or a friend. Of course she is lonely. Then comes the oft-repeated temptation that the devil has planned is forced upon her, and she makes the acquaintance of a stranger who does not care, only to ruin her. And then who is there to take care? She is a stranger in a strange city, her loved ones are far away and anyway the awful thought of disgracing her father's home haunts her until the suggestion to end it all comes. She can make her way through the dark to the edge of the Saskatchewan [river] to end her misery, and who cares if she does? ... I have listened to stories like this more than once ... These young girls come in from a homestead to take work in a hotel or café where they can earn good wages. Are they attacked? Oh no, the agent of evil comes along and tells them they can earn more money and have nicer clothes and possess jewelry and many of these poor ignorant girls consent to have more money and fine clothes and jewelry at the cost of the most sacred endowment God could bestow on a woman. ("Fallen and unfortunate women," n.d. but probably 1911, PR0803)

Without intervention, the girl who had "fallen" could be headed for an even worse fate, as a prostitute:

> The young mother is left with one or more children to support. Under this burden the pressure of temptation comes. It is sharp and keen. She loves her babies and desires to provide for them. The temptation often overcomes her and she becomes a victim of a life far worse than poverty ... Their life of only five years in the [illegible] pool of this evil is worse than a thousand deaths. Oh the horror of those years. Cut off from loved ones, she would not for the world let her people know and she feels no one cares. So she suffers and suffers a slave and diseased, her only prospect is death. Soon she will hear that fateful sentence: "She that is [illegible] let

her be [illegible] still, and she that is filthy, let her be filthy still." Soon she will be lying where so many others have lain, in a morgue, awaiting a pauper's funeral. ("Rescue work in Edmonton," handwritten, n.d. but probably 1909, PR0803)

Only through careful and altruistic investment of time, money, dedication, and spiritual grace could the fallen girl regain the virtue she had lost. On the fifth anniversary of the home, the chief matron wrote exultantly in her address to the attendees:

Sometimes there is a letter that comes back after [a client] has gone her way into the world, full of penitence, that rejoices the heart of the workers … Some are in homes of their own or among their own people. Others are among strangers and living a Christlike life. If you could hear some of the prayers of thanksgiving to God for such a Home that we have heard and read some letters that we have safely placed away as a prize, you would say with us that the triumphs of rescue work are glorious indeed.

Advocates at Beulah were emphatic that client-saving was a form of investment, in which emotion, time, and spiritual grace would turn a profit:

What does it pay to make all this sacrifice for the unfortunate girl? It is true she has been robbed of the priceless treasure of woman's virtue, she has fallen among thieves who have wounded her, robbed her and left her half dead: she is an expectant mother and must face the unspeakable sorrow of bringing into the world a nameless babe … We have all confidence in the old gospel and its power to transform and to completely restore. There is not only hope, but the possibility of a noble and useful life. ("Twenty-Five Years of Rescue Work at Beulah Home," 17, PR0803)

Beulah representatives, especially when addressing faith-based audiences, turned this narrative into a profoundly gendered economy of prodigality, expenditure, and the replenishment of moral capital, suggesting that the clients of Beulah, because they were women, were both more vulnerable to the loss of virtue and more able to attain a greater level of moral virtue than "fallen" men:

Some may ask – why the effort? Why spend money, time and lives? Why not work for the protection of the pure girl? Why give all the attention to

the prodigal girl? Here is the answer. Did you ever notice that it is only one gospel records the story of the prodigal boy. He deliberately went astray [and was] glad he went home [and] received a welcome, ring, robe, fatted calf and a merry time. No mention of his name or what he did afterwards. The prodigal girl [Mary Magdalene] is down too, but enticed away. All the four gospels record it and give her name. She was so lost that seven devils possessed her. Was she redeemed? Yes [she was] first at the tomb, sent by the risen Christ to tell the disciples of his resurrection, the first messenger of the glorious truth. Do you wonder why we do it now?
(typescript speech titled "Sunday January 25 1914," PR0803)

The image of Mary Magdalene recurred in Beulah materials. While other maternity homes also used the Magdalene as a symbol of sin and/or forgiveness, in Beulah discourse she was a stand-in for girls who had been robbed of all their virtue, like the prodigal son and his wealth, but who went on to regain far more than they had lost, in the form of spiritual grace. The story of the Magdalene's witness to the risen Christ was used to demonstrate that the kindness and compassion that Jesus showed the fallen woman paid off abundantly through her elevation to timeless sanctity; and that by analogy, investment in the Magdalenes of Edmonton would reap abundant rewards.

Was this hegemonic narrative of "girl-mothers" seduced and abandoned typical of the real experiences of women who came to Beulah? Their own accounts are lost, but case files from the provincial agents responsible for enforcing the Children of Unmarried Parents Act (CUPA), which required men to assume the costs of children they had fathered out of wedlock, including paying for their stay at Beulah, suggest a much wider range of experiences. The situations in these case files cover everything from consensual relations between partners in a committed relationship to frank rape, with very little mention of the classic Beulah narrative. Two examples illustrate this diversity. The first is a witness statement from a woman who employed the pregnant woman as a domestic worker:

I first employed [woman's name] as a domestic in 1922 ... During that time she did not keep company with anyone but [the putative father], not to my knowledge anyway. Her baby was born November 1924 ... [He] brought her a wristwatch. I scolded her very much for taking it, not being engaged to him. I don't remember ever seeing him again until the Sunday following my birthday between one and two o'clock in the morning ... I saw [him] in front of the kitchen table and I screamed, not expecting to see a man in the house and I asked [woman's name] what was the man doing there and why she had gone upstairs. She said she had gone to get a letter to mail to her sister who was in the isolation ward with diphtheria. That was the night it occurred ... I never noticed her keeping company with [him] after that occasion. She may have gone out with him once or twice but not to my knowledge. I knew absolutely nothing of her condition until she told me in May of this year. I have nothing but the very best to say of the girl's behaviour. (Children of Unwed Parents Act, Sept 14/23–Dec31/25, PAA 75.146 3342a, box 174, 12C5)

The second is an account by a different woman, who was making a paternity claim:

In January 1924 [putative father] came to see me at my house. My father and mother had gone to my sister's place. I was alone in the house. [He] stayed all day and about 10.00 at night I was upstairs, Xxx followed me upstairs and threw me on the bed and forced me to have sexual intercourse with him. After this occurred he told me not to say anything to anyone and he would marry me after Easter. He continued to come to see me at my house and about a month after he forced me he again had sexual intercourse with me. On this occasion also my father and mother were away from home ... He was coming to see me all the time and on each occasion when my mother and father were away from home he had sexual intercourse with me. He promised each time to marry me and said if we would make a baby we would get married quicker. About the middle of June 1924 I found I was pregnant. When I found the condition I was in I told [him] and he said I should not get scared or bothered and that he would marry me. On the 7th of January 1925 [he] was at our place and told me that as soon as the holidays were past we would go to Smoky Lake and get married. I have not seen [him] since that date. (Children of Unwed Parents Act, Sept 14/23-Dec31/25, PAA 75.146 3342a, box 174, 12C5)

Almost none of the cases in the CUPA files follow the dominant Beulah narrative, which is not surprising. In developing an economy of virtue surrounding unmarried pregnant women, iconic images and affect-laden representations of young girls who had lost their most precious treasures were better currency than accounts of actual pregnancies.

If Beulah's clients had lost their virtue and the precious treasure of their womanhood, Beulah would help them reaccumulate it, even as it provided pragmatic help with the logistics of pregnancy and birth. The primary way in which these young women could redeem their virtue was through religious commitment. Indeed, one of the main activities at the Home was Christian evangelism. Early annual reports, although inconsistent in format, record the number of "girls professing conversion" (21 in 1914) and the number of religious services held (104 in 1924) as well as the number of clients admitted and babies born. Beulah routines included daily prayer meetings as well as formal church services and Sunday school once a week, and one of the visiting pastors, from the Moravian church, noted approvingly that "it will be utterly well with [Beulah clients] if their spirit will bow in abject obedience of faith at the feet of the savior of men" ("Twenty-Five Years of Rescue Work: Beulah Home 1909–1919").

The Beulah administration collected and reprinted in fundraising documents many letters they had received from former residents that expressed a spiritual gratitude, suggesting the magnitude of the efforts to bring the "girls" to Jesus. These letters include references to the relief of the writer's "sin-sick soul" by their conversion experience at Beulah, and their gratitude at being brought to Christianity.[5] One former client's letter was quoted in the 1932 anniversary report:

> Many like myself may have been taught the story of Jesus in childhood but ... let unbelief and doubt creep into their hearts ... But ... from the scriptural lessons taught here in the Home belief in the Bible and salvation has been restored to me. (typescript titled "1932 anniversary speech," PR 0803)

Alongside religion, however, there was an arguably equally powerful process for restoring value to clients. This was through the deployment of domesticity in Beulah, through the passing on of gender-appropriate housekeeping skills and the replaying of normative familiality, especially normative mother–daughter relations, in symbolic form. The physical and interpersonal environments were strategically manipulated to create an archetypal home, an engine of replenishment and rejuvenation for women who had lost their most valuable possessions.

The tremendous faith that Beulah staff placed in the transformative strength of "hominess" was typical of maternity homes of the day. The Crittenden Homes, the largest chain of such facilities in the United States, were founded on a belief in "the redemptive power of domesticity," which was thought to be "curative for women who had flouted domestic conventions" by non-marital sex (Kunzel 1995). In Toronto, managers of homes of very different religious denominations took a common pride in the "homelikeness" and "family atmosphere" of their institutions (Murray 2004, 260).

At Beulah, domesticity was equated with light and redemption. When a permanent facility was built on what was then the outskirts of Edmonton, newspapers gushed over the coziness and charm of the home:

> Sunlight floods the Beulah Home north of the city … Just how the architect managed to get so many windows facing south is hard to tell. He must have had in mind the nature of the work to be carried on there and the need of plenty of brightness and sunshine. And the nursery where five tiny babies sleep and eat and cry and sleep some more is sunniest of all, and spotlessly clean. These conditions exist throughout the home, and if a clean bright environment has any influence on a disheartened or careless girl, that influence working silently in the Beulah home is a strong one. (clipping titled "A home which tries to rectify the unnamed sins of society," n.d. but probably 1909, PR 0803)

And on the occasion of Beulah's fifth anniversary:

> The Beulah home is an ideal place in an ideal spot and one can hardly imagine a more homelike shelter for the girls. The large sunny rooms, the two verandahs, the two acres of ground, the conservatory and the pretty furnishings throughout tend to develop the love of a quiet, pretty home and are indeed a revelation to many of the girls who have never had a chance to grow in a domestic atmosphere. (clipping titled "Beulah mission established five years ago does good work among the fallen ones," n.d. but probably 1914, PR0803)

Clients were trained in the domestic arts of cooking, cleaning, and decorating, partly as vocational preparation for domestic service (which was often presumed to be the destiny of Beulah clients who did not marry), and partly for the morally regenerative effects of housekeeping:

> The rooms are bright, cozy and spotlessly clean, a splendid recommendation for the girls who come away to seek employment after a few months' shelter under its roof … Those who are not good housekeepers when they enter cannot fail to learn the art under the care of Miss Chatham and her

helpers (clipping titled "Beulah rescue mission holds celebration, over 100 attend," n.d. but probably 1919, PR0803)

Even more important than the physical effects of domesticity was the replaying of familial relations. It was presumed that clients' parenting and family relationships had not been adequate and that Beulah would be their first encounter with normative family life. In effect, the "girl-mothers" were returned to a state of fictive childhood, where the deficiencies in their original formation could be remedied through an accelerated immersion in both the spiritual and the practical work of Christian family life:

> There in an atmosphere of love and sympathy, they are sheltered and cared for, and in a real Christian home – often their first experience of such surroundings – they are given a new vision of life. So effective is this morally that in very few cases does the girl[] sink back into the old life. (clipping titled "Where girls find help," n.d. but probably 1919, PR0803)

In superintendents' reports to the board of directors and in speeches and texts prepared for supporters, Beulah was constantly referred to as a "family," with the births of new babies duly noted as "additions to our Beulah family." Clients were encouraged to think of one another as "sisters," and Beulah often quoted letters from former clients who were nostalgic for the "family" they had found at the home. The superintendent, the matron, and the nursing staff were positioned as surrogate mothers who could provide the love and guidance that the clients had been deprived of as daughters:

> Many of the girls who come to the home ... become mothers when they themselves were most in need of a mother's protection. How different their lives might have been had they had a mother's love and careful supervision! ("Some sad stories from Beulah Home," in *Twenty-Five Years of Rescue Work: Beulah Home 1909–1936*, 21, PR0803)

Beulah could stand in as a second mother for such girls, but the absence of appropriate maternal guidance could never be entirely recuperated:

> This stream of broken girlhood is so sad. How we would like to grant a full and gracious release and return these little girls to their parents and

friends without even a memory of so sad a chapter in their past. ("1928 anniversary report," n.p., PR0803)

Although "so sad a chapter" could never be completely erased, at Beulah the investments in the clients of spiritual guidance and recuperative domesticity paid dividends. These dividends were noted in the Beulah files in the form of girls who regained their feminine value, primarily by marrying and having their own families, but also by living useful lives caring for others. Weddings of former Beulah clients were always prominently noted in annual reports (with care taken to preserve the anonymity of the bride), and as early as 1912, some former clients held their weddings at Beulah, with the virginal trappings of wedding gowns and veils. In 1926, the annual report noted approvingly that "indeed we have a fine record of at least 25% of our girls being married in the past five years." Stories of girls who married respectably, or who took up caring professions such as nursing or teaching, were often inserted into newspaper articles and documents produced by Beulah. Several former clients went on to missionary work in Canada and abroad. A promotional piece from the 1930s, purportedly consisting of extracts from letters written by former clients, informed supporters that

> in the past six years, 292 young women have been at Beulah Home. Today 31% are married and living in established homes; 53% are living with their parents or earning a living in some honest way; three per cent are unknown at present, and only five per cent have not made as good as we would wish to see, the other eight percent make up the present family [i.e., are presently living at Beulah]. (typescript speech titled "That bundle of letters," n.d. but probably 1935, PR0803)

The redemption of these clients marked the full cycle of the economy of virtue at Beulah – virtue as a feminine form of wealth that was the birthright of all women, that was lost or stolen and then re-created and redistributed to those from whom it had been dispossessed, through careful investments in spirituality and domesticity.

An Economy of Babies

If the notion of an economy of virtue seems somewhat abstract, the economy of bodies at Beulah was solidly corporeal – sometimes distressingly so – to twenty-first-century sensibilities. The main units of value in this economy were the "little treasures," that is, the babies born to Beulah clients. Economic metaphors are unavoidable in describing the distribution and circulation of these infant resources, which sometimes took the form of something very close to a market.

In the early years of Beulah, babies were in surplus. Some babies, as noted earlier, were boarded at Beulah by their biological mothers until the mothers were able to retrieve them, but the real problem was babies awaiting adoption, who could remain at Beulah for a year or more. Newspaper articles emphasized the overabundance of infants at the home and promoted funding drives to extend the nursery facilities so that more adoptable babies could be accommodated and not transferred as quickly into the provincial foster care system, which was widely acknowledged to be underregulated and haphazard. One 1924 article likened the staff of Beulah to "the famous old woman who lived in a shoe [and had so many babies, she didn't know what to do]" (clipping of same title, n.d. but probably 1924, PR0803).

To find homes for these babies, Beulah and its supporters advertised the children, stressing their beauty, winsomeness, and capacity to give affection. A major annual event at Beulah was the anniversary open day, during which visitors were encouraged to tour the nurseries. The babies on display were visibly divided into those that were available for adoption and those that were not, by means of tags attached to cribs or to the infants themselves. The local newspapers faithfully covered the open day, promoting the event in advance and describing the attractive babies on offer:

> The nurseries were fresh and attractive with their aquamarine tinted walls and their bunny-designed curtains. Here were the babies, some sleeping peacefully through all the excitement, other protesting loudly, some just indifferent. Like dainty flowers they were dressed in palest pink, green and blue, and a winsome dark eyed Japanese baby was adorable in canary yellow ... But upon many of the cribs was the poignant printed statement: I am for adoption. (clipping titled "More babies adopted from Beulah Home," 14 September 1936, PR0803)

Individual babies were also singled out by their attractiveness:

> Belle has blue eyes and a lot of that sub-bronze red hair that is after all the last word in feminine beauty and she has the happiest disposition imaginable. From her cot in the sunny baby cottage, Belle gurgles and coos and

looks with bright eyes at passersby. In her own particular language she is saying "please missus, I'd love to come to your house and make you realize just what a treasure I am." Belle is just one of ten babies who are for adoption at Beulah Home at this time. (clipping titled "Redheaded baby would like to win parents," n.d. but probably 1930, PR0803)

The desires of parents for adoptable babies, as well as the desires of the babies for parents, were discursively and affectively mobilized to drive the circulation and redistribution of children. Empty maternal hearts were described as filled by the adoption of a baby, and fatherly pleasures in the hijinks of children were gratified through adoption:

Dimples and baby smiles, blue eyes and brown, is it any wonder that almost any day one may see a car drawn up at the doors of the Beulah home while some woman is satisfying the hunger of her heart and some man is enjoying the instinctive pride of fatherhood when such babies as those at the home can be adopted for keeps? (clipping titled "Beulah Home builds again," n.d. but probably 1928, PR0803)

The investment in adoption was sure to pay dividends, not only in the private joy that babies brought to the family but also in the creation of useful public citizens. In the 1940s, when the first "generation" of babies born at Beulah had grown to adulthood, advertisements from Hill's office and promotional material from Beulah noted that Beulah babies were now serving their communities as businessmen, Sunday school teachers, successful farmers, and so forth. In a 1944 typescript for an address to the Community Chest, special mention was made of Beulah boys now serving in the army (PR 1971.007 – 1, Beulah Home, "Questions and answers for Community Chest 1944").

All the babies were described as "treasures" and "precious," but some evidently commanded higher value than others. Most notably, girl babies were more desirable to prospective parents than boys, so that on open days

sturdy boy babies kick their legs and coo to no account, so long as the adjoining crib holds a girl baby. This is one of the few instances where the girls have the advantage ... It is strange that no one wants a boy baby. Every prospective adopter wants blue-eyed girls and the homes cannot keep up with the demand for these fair maidens. Yet Robbie and Billie,

Tommie, Danny, Jack and two others are bonnie babies and express their willingness to do their part if only someone will have them. (clipping titled "Sixteen babies rejoice: Beulah home nursery completed," n.d. but probably 1923, PR0803)

While gender evidently stratified babies' attractiveness to prospective parents, racial or ethnic background did not appear to stratify the babies. As noted above, babies with Asian parentage were described as "winsome" and "dainty," while babies with African parentage were similarly exoticized, in terms that grate on present-day sensibilities:

One of our treasures is a chocolate baby girl with big black eyes and a kinky curly head. She is learning to swing and an order has been sent in for a swing set. (1930 Christmas card to supporters, PR0803)

In 1948, an appeal to donors claimed that

there's no racial discrimination for babies at the Beulah Home. Babies of all races and nationalities will have a happy life … [For instance] Dovie, a pretty negro child of eight and a half months, will have a better start in life if our coffers are filled. (clipping titled "These bright Beulah Home babies need Community Chest support," n.d., PR0803)

Aboriginal children were never mentioned, and the staffers at Beulah appear to have been oblivious to the existence of Edmonton's growing urban Aboriginal population.[6] Similarly, the existence of infants with disabilities or who were less than physically perfect was never mentioned.

In the 1930s and 1940s, the number of adoptable babies at Beulah was rising sharply, largely due to the Depression, which was forcing families off farms and young women into employment and precarious autonomy in Edmonton; later, the garrisoning of American troops in Edmonton resulted in greater possibilities for non-marital sex and pregnancy. In addition, as the Depression took hold some women who had been boarding their babies at Beulah were no longer able to afford the $5 weekly charge, and released the baby for adoption. These same conditions also led to a decrease in the demand for adoptable babies: in times of economic uncertainty, marriages were being postponed, and potential parents were more reluctant to bring a child into their family.

As a result, the effort to "sell" Beulah babies to the public was ratcheted up several notches, and the babies were advertised as delightful additions to households.

This intensification owed much to the interventions of Charles "Uncle Charlie" Hill, a child welfare inspector since 1923 who made his way to the top of the bureaucratic hierarchy as Superintendent of Child Welfare in the 1940s, and who had strong ties to Beulah in his professional capacity and as a volunteer member of the board of directors. Hill was a flamboyant and controversial figure whose aggressive approach to "placing out" adoptable children led to an apparent commercialization of adoptive parenting and of the babies themselves. Hill spearheaded promotional campaigns such as annual "adopt-a-baby weeks" from the 1930s onwards, promoting Beulah children in the same way that other businessmen promoted their wares.

For Hill, Beulah was a reliable source of babies of known parentage, professionally cared for and meeting standards of desirability, as distinct from the other children who came under his care through abandonment, neglect, or facilities for the delinquent. Accounts of his term as superintendent suggest that he personally signed off on the adoptions of 12,000 children. It is not clear how much of this volume of business came from Beulah, but certainly the great majority of Beulah adoptions went through Hill, and the home was one of his promotional showplaces.

A 1938 newspaper article titled "Baby adoption a Christmas gift idea" urged readers:

How about doing part of your Christmas shopping in the basement of the Legislative Building [where the provincial child welfare offices were located] this year? ... "What could make a grander Christmas present than a darling baby?" Mr. Hill asks, revealing that he now has for adoption some of the finest babies he has ever seen in his 24 years as official "baby man" for the provincial government. (clipping, n.d., November 1938, PR0803)

Two years later, the stock of available babies was even larger, and Hill was telling the newspapers that he intended to place thirty babies in thirty homes in one week:

[Hill] wants to place those 30 babies in 30 good homes and is sure they will go fast. Because this year Mr. Hill says he has just about the finest assortment of babies on hand he has ever seen and he has been in the baby business for a good many years. Who knows? Perhaps in this collection there is the future prime minister of Canada or the president of the CPR ... He is anxious to show his present stock-in-trade and is certain that one look at any of the present supply will win a prospective parents' heart. (clipping titled "30 babies wait for homes," n.d. but probably December 1940, PR0803)

Hill also emphasized that the babies could be taken "on trial" and returned or exchanged if they proved unsatisfactory or showed evidence of any hereditary defects.

Hill's style was also evident in gimmicks such as the "Silver Seven" – seven infants chosen to be advertised in the Edmonton newspapers in the weeks leading up to Christmas, with exhortations to readers to "make themselves the best Christmas present." The babies were named and photographed and thereby personalized for readers:

Merry Christmas, folks! We know it's a little early, but how's chances to spend Christmas with you? We'd like to hang our little pink and blue sox on somebody's mantelpiece and have a real Christmas in a real home of our own with a real mummy and daddy ... That's the Silver Seven, Mr. and Mrs. Edmonton. All they want is a home and a daddy and a mummy. It doesn't have to be a wealthy home, just a home where they'll be appreciated and pay it back some time with brimful and overflowing, with love and affection. Just call ... [and] you can make yourself the best Christmas present anyone could give you – one of these sturdy little Canadians. (clipping titled "Orphans! We want a home," n.d. but probably November 1945, PR0803)

It is impossible to say how the Beulah staff reacted to the marketing of their infants. However, those staff lent their names and images to articles and brochures about Hill's programs, celebrating the success of Alberta's baby exports. Hill claimed that "letters come from all over Canada and the US asking to adopt babies," and Finlay concurred that "many of our children are adopted by American couples. Only this week a baby boy left for California with his new parents ... and we received a picture and a glowing account of one of the babies who was adopted by a home in Nevada" (clipping titled "Mrs. M Finlay, foster mother to babies at Beulah Home," 28 September 1945, PR0803). In a fundraising brochure from the late 1940s, the attractiveness of Beulah babies on the international adoption circuit was similarly stressed, through quotes from letters from American adopting parents:

3.1 Advertising seven adoptable babies for Christmas. The article at the foot of the page reads in part: "How about giving yourself a real Christmas present this year? One that will make the Christmas season of 1938 a 'stand out' in your life from now on? A present that will pay real dividends down through the years in love and affection, the kind that only a real boy can give. ... So how about it, you men and women who have been thinking about adopting a baby boy? Take Mr Hill's word for it: They are the 'pick of the basket' and won't last long."

Source: *Edmonton Bulletin*, 19 November 1938, 1.

My trip to Edmonton seems just like a dream ... I can think of nothing but praise for the Canadian people and my children will never be ashamed of having come from your great country ... I certainly was impressed by your Beulah Home, the place where we found our children.

Satisfied beyond words! We have a little child from the Beulah Home and the joy we have already experienced has been far beyond our expectation and we are sure this little life will turn many lonely hours into joyous ones. (pamphlet titled "A memento of Beulah Home," n.d. but probably 1947, PR0803)

However, in 1948, the high-turnover, high-volume economy of babies in Alberta was dealt a huge blow by an investigation into child welfare in the province, conducted by Charlotte Whitton (then a muckraking journalist, later the first woman mayor of Ottawa) at the behest of the Imperial Order Daughters of the Empire, whose members worried that child welfare services in general were underregulated and were being run as personal fiefdoms. Whitton uncovered plenty of evidence that child welfare services were being mismanaged, but the biggest bombshell in her report involved allegations that highly placed bureaucrats in child welfare were taking cash for adoptions, turning the metaphorical baby market into a literal market, a source of financial profit.[7] Hill was not named directly in the report, but given his centrality in adoptions, he was clearly the target of the allegations.

Whitton alleged that Americans, particularly in the border states, were arranging international adoptions, including the provision of passports for infants, entirely by mail, with no oversight of the adoptive homes and no vetting of the prospective adoptive parents. Babies could be picked up in Edmonton or even delivered directly to their new homes by couriers from Alberta. Whitton also speculated on the existence of a secondary black market in babies in the United States, into which Albertan babies were being drawn by middlemen posing as potential adopters. Whitton's report was wildly controversial in Alberta and attracted international attention. *Time Magazine* described her as "one of the most determined women in the Dominion [of Canada]" and cast her as David to Charlie Hill's Goliath ("Determined woman," *Time*, 4 August 1947).

Whitton was clearly attuned to the circulation of adoptable babies as an economic matter, writing that "if these babies are suitable for adoption, they are a valuable national asset and the whole Alberta policy [of expediting adoptions to the United States] is puzzling; if they are not suitable for placement, it is a dastardly thing to send them to foster [and adoptive] homes in a friendly neighboring country" (ibid.).

The provincial government held a commission of inquiry into the allegations in the Whitton/IODE report and, perhaps not surprisingly, found that there was no solid evidence of babies being sold. Nonetheless, the Howson Commission concluded that cross-border adoptions should be terminated. Staff from Beulah Home gave testimony at the inquiry, stating that their role in the circulation of adoptable babies was founded in compassion and empathy for birth mothers. They stated that mothers were never pressured to sign over their valuable infants for adoption, and that furthermore Beulah had never received advice or instructions from the provincial government about how to increase the number of babies available for adoption.

With the cross-border baby-selling scandal, the hard-sell approach to the distribution of Beulah babies came to an end. Newspapers continued to run pictures of adorable infants in their best clothes, who would "be at home to visitors to the nursery" every year on Beulah's open days (photo caption, n.d. but probably 1957). However, the adopt-a-baby weeks and the Silver Seven mode of distributing children had come to a close. As the volume of adoptable infants declined through the 1960s, both because more mothers were keeping their infants and because more were giving birth in standard hospitals rather than Beulah's specialized facilities, the economy of babies became less fraught and more standardized within the provincial bureaucracy.

Conclusion

The economy of virtue and the economy of babies shaped the experiences of women and infants whose lives intersected with the Beulah Home. The women's virtue, a gendered symbolic resource, was understood as something that could be illicitly taken from girls through theft and fraud. However, this loss could be recouped through careful investment of time, prayer, compassion, and donations, generating spiritual and psychological dividends for both the individual and her society. The consequence of that loss of virtue, the baby, was subject to market forces bound up with the fluctuations of supply and demand over the decades, and caught up in processes of distribution that often veered perilously close to commodification.

The relationships between these economies are complex and not always self-evident. The most obvious form of relation is isomorphism, in that pregnant women and adoptable babies were imagined in structurally similar ways. Both the women and the babies existed outside of normative families, and both women and babies were positioned as minors in need of rescue and maternal love in order to transform their lives and recuperate them. Both babies and mothers had the potential to overcome unsuccessful beginnings and become valuable members of society as a consequence of the kindness they encountered at Beulah. The power of this positioning of the "child-mothers" was such that it persisted even when other evidence of the women's lives, such as their ages or the details of the experiences that had led them to become pregnant, contradicted the view of them as hapless children.

However, the more profound relationship between the two economies is more alchemical than isomorphic. The babies, adorable and adoptable, were a transfiguration of the tragedies that had attended their coming into being. In the imaginative discourse of Beulah, the depletion of virtue, the depletion of feminine treasure through non-marital sex, was transformed into another kind of treasure, in the form of babies. The loss of virtue was thus converted into something of tremendous value – a baby. These infant treasures could not exist without the loss of their mother's greatest treasure, her feminine virtue. In this way, the abject dross of the seduced and deceived woman became the golden treasure of the baby (sometimes almost literally golden, if the rumours of baby-selling have any validity). The intrinsic value of these babies to hopeful adoptive parents, to Charlie Hill, and as precious individuals within the Christian ethos of Beulah, approached if it did not surpass the loss of value experienced by their mothers when they became pregnant without marriage. Babies and feminine virtue were acquired, depleted, distributed, and transformed one into the other.

4 Mothers' Duties: Eugenics, Sterilization, and the United Farm Women of Alberta

Introduction

Illegitimate births were not the only births that troubled Albertans in the early years of the province. In this chapter we turn to consider another category of such births. These births were troubling not because of the circumstances in which they occurred but because of the mothers (and to a lesser degree, the fathers) who were involved. These were the births to the "feeble-minded" or the "undesirable," those who ought not to reproduce but who might do so anyway. The fear and anxiety occasioned by these births was directly responsible for one of the worst human rights violations in Canadian history.

In 1928 the government of Alberta enacted the Sexual Sterilization Act, providing for the permanent sterilization of men and women in provincial psychiatric institutions. In 1972 the abolition of this act was the first legislative act of the incoming Progressive Conservative government under Peter Lougheed. In the intervening years, more than 2,800 people were sterilized. The Alberta program was one of the most extensive in the world. During the 1930s, the Alberta government carried out 12.8 female sterilizations per 100,000 population per year, placing it just behind the American state of Virginia, with 13.42 per 100,000 per year (Grekul, Krahn, and Odynak 2004, 357). In future decades, the rate of female sterilization slowed down, but Alberta still had the highest or second-highest rates for any jurisdiction in North America. Even during the 1960s, Alberta was still sterilizing 8.06 people per 100,000 per year, well ahead of second-place North Carolina with 4.24 (ibid.).

Alberta's sterilization program is now universally condemned as a violation of human rights and as an abuse of state power. A representative of the Lougheed government, which repealed the act in 1972, described it as "a reprehensible and intolerable philosophy and program for this province" (in Caulfield and Robertson 1996, 65; see also Cairney 1996, Wahlsten 1997).

Yet just a generation earlier, prominent interest groups had been eager to claim the Sexual Sterilization Act as a triumph for Alberta women. In her 1944 booklet "Thirty Years of Progress: History of the United Farm Women of Alberta," Eva Carter wrote: "To the United Farm Women of Alberta is given the credit for the most advanced piece of legislation ever to be enacted in Alberta: the placing on the statute books of the Sexual Sterilization Act, and later amendments giving wider powers to the Act" (PAA, PR1971.420, box 2, file 31).

How did sexual sterilization come to be seen as the apex of "advanced legislation" in Alberta, rather than an indefensible act of hubris as it appears today? How did Albertans, primarily but not exclusively women, come to advocate sterilization as not only justifiable but also humane and reasonable? And why were women, who bore the brunt of the act, the strongest advocates for sterilization during the grim decades of the 1910s and 1920s?

In this chapter I attempt to answer these questions by exploring the broader context of eugenics, the context in which this now-notorious piece of legislation could have been understood as a victory for women. I do not deal directly with the enactment, the consequences, or the later repeal of the act, for that territory has already been ably covered by others (Chapman 1977; Grekul 2002, 2008; Grekul, Krahn, and Odynak 2004). Erika Dyck (2013) provides the most comprehensive account of the full multi-decade sweep of eugenics in Alberta, including the men and women who were sterilized as well as the multitude of players in the eugenic enterprise. My focus here is much narrower: I am concerned with the interwar era – the decades to either side of the act – and with the ways in which sterilization was understood by its most ardent proponents, the mothers and wives who made up Alberta's women's organizations, including the extremely influential United Farm Women of Alberta (UFWA). These organizations worked to shape how, when, and to whom children would be born. I examine the social imaginary that formed the crucible for this drive to solve social problems through reproductive means, with particular attention to the imbrications of gender, in both overt and subtle manifestations.

Most of the statistical information related to the sterilization era in Alberta has been destroyed or is barred to researchers under privacy laws. Nonetheless, Dyck (2013), Grekul (2008) and Grekul and colleagues (2004) have already done an excellent job of quantifying and describing trends in sterilization in Alberta based on what little information is accessible, and Christian (1974), Puplampu (2008), and Wahlsten (1997) have written about the circumstances under which sterilization was ended in the 1970s, and about the limited redress provided to its survivors in the 1990s. Here, I focus on a small slice of time and on a particular imaginative economy of reproduction that prevailed in the 1920s, linked with but not reducible to the political economy of Alberta. Understanding this imaginative economy is the key to answering the question posed at the beginning of this chapter: How did sexual sterilization make sense? In particular, how did it make sense to *women*?

"Positive" and "Negative" Eugenics

The rise of eugenic sterilization in the early decades of the twentieth century was a global phenomenon. In most histories, the eugenics movements of the twentieth century are portrayed as triumphalist endeavours to create a race of newer, better human beings, purged of defect and weakness. These movements, whether in the United States, France, Australia, Sweden, or (most notoriously) Germany, are depicted as a product of arrogance, racism, and bad science, cloaked by assertions about patriotism and human perfectibility. This approach to eugenics as the perfection of the human race had both a "positive" side – encouraging more births from people considered to be of good stock – and a "negative" side – discouraging, prohibiting, or punishing the reproduction of people considered less desirable.

"Positive" eugenics included initiatives such as marriage bureaux, pro-fertility campaigns aimed at particular groups of eugenically desirable individuals, and competitions for the best pedigrees or the most eugenically perfect children. Negative eugenics meant prohibition, not encouragement. Some eugenics programs attempted to prohibit "dysgenic" marriages between individuals with undesirable traits, but regulating marriage and sexual relations was a tricky and inefficient way to regulate reproduction. The most extreme form of negative eugenics was the direct prevention of reproduction, through surgical sterilization of men and women who were deemed by state authorities to be a dysgenic threat to the community (Bashford and Levine 2010 provide a comprehensive overview of negative and positive eugenics in the twentieth century).

"High" and "Low" Eugenics

Both negative and positive modalities of eugenics were the cornerstone of state projects intended to create a superior race or nation. The title of Angus McLaren's seminal work on eugenics in Canada, *Our Own Master Race* (1990), closely reflects this view of eugenic history, as does the title of Edwin Black's bestselling treatise on American eugenics, *War Against the Weak: America's Campaign to Create a Master Race* (2003). Regarding Alberta, however, I argue that the story of eugenics as a vainglorious project to transform the human race offers only a partial understanding of how ordinary women, as well as philosophically inclined elites, came to support negative eugenics and sterilization. My argument is premised on the idea that there were multiple eugenic logics at work. In particular, I draw a distinction between what I call a "high" narrative of eugenics in which these projects and the philosophies behind them were understood as the products of beliefs about science, perfectibility, and the triumphs of certain types of people over others; and a "low" narrative of eugenics, in which support for negative eugenic policies was grounded in pessimistic perceptions of society.

This distinction is not hard and fast. Many supporters of "high" eugenics, envisaging a future of perfect human beings, also harnessed the rhetoric and ideas of "low" eugenics, in which eugenic measures were seen as coping measures for social failures. Histories of eugenics in Canada, such as those by McLaren (1990), Dyck (2013), and Dowbiggin (1997), have shown that "high" eugenic dreams of creating a better breed of humans, "purified" of all heritable taint, coexisted with "low" eugenic preoccupations with the failures and miseries of contemporary life. The eugenic enterprise in Alberta was similar. It borrowed from different sources and philosophies about progress, sex, and social welfare. That said, the weight of eugenic arguments was located more in the "low" register, drawing on women's perceptions that Alberta was struggling against a tide of problems for which eugenic measures might provide partial relief, than in the "high" register. The grand expectations of a new society were a secondary theme in the debates conducted by women's organizations promoting sexual sterilization – debates that had much to do with the grinding miseries of the 1920s. Eugenic measures, including sterilization, were seen as a remedy for social ills that no other measures had been able to address.

In "low" eugenic discourse, the eugenic project was not about creating a future race of "human thoroughbreds" (McLaren 1990, 91) but about compensating for the failures of the present social order, which were yielding up human misery. "Low" eugenics was marked by efforts at recuperation, at staving off disaster. The watchwords of "high" eugenics included such terms as "triumph," "victory," and "superior"; the watchwords of "low" eugenics included such terms as "failure," "danger," and "fear." This discourse of "low" eugenics is similar to the discourse of "white trash" explored by Nicole Hahn Rafter (1988a). She points out that the eugenic programs in the United States (often cited and referred to by Alberta's eugenicists) were not always motivated by inspiring visions of a world filled with "human thoroughbreds"; also in circulation was the dystopian prospect of a world filled with people who were the antithesis of thoroughbreds. Rafter writes that many American eugenicists "had little confidence in the survival of the fittest; what worried them was the survival of the unfit" (Rafter 1988b, 44).

Often slighted in these discussions of "white trash" and "unfit propagators," however, is the element of charitable concern for those people who were targeted for sterilization. I do not intend to portray the eugenicists of the UFWA as kind altruists or as kindly disposed towards the indigent or marginalized people around them. Expressions of disdain for or fear of such people were woven through the advocacy and lobbying for sterilization. Nonetheless, as I show below, the justifications for sterilization did include some measure of compassion for the people being sterilized, and there were glimmerings of concern for the ill-treatment to which women of limited cognitive capacity were subjected by the men around them.

The narrative of "high" eugenics has often been used to frame discussions of eugenic policies and practices in the twentieth century, partly because the acknowledged "fathers" of the movement, such as Francis Galton, had a nineteenth-century optimism about human progress and evolution towards a higher end, inflected both by Christian teleology and by the new science of evolution. This optimism was even evident in the popular poetry and literature of the day, as in British poet laureate Alfred Lord Tennyson's epic poem *In Memoriam*, in which the narrator, lamenting the death of a close friend, is comforted by a vision of a glorious future for humanity as a whole, "towards which the whole creation moves."

Galton saw eugenics as a means to an end of racial uplift, "improving human stock by giving the more suitable races or strains of blood an opportunity to prevail" (Galton 1883, 24, in Barrett and Kurzman 2004, 497). His American disciple, Charles Davenport, who created the influential American Eugenics Record Office in 1910, called eugenics "the science of the improvement of the human race through better breeding" (Davenport 1911, 1, in Allen 1986, 225). At the inaugural First National Conference on Race Betterment, held in Michigan in 1914, J.H. Kellogg (of the Kellogg's Corn Flakes family) called for nothing less than "a new human race" (Kellogg 1914, cited in Selden 2005, 224). With such a triumphalist heritage (followed by such a disastrous downfall in Nazi Germany), it is not surprising that historians of eugenics have tended to emphasize the grandiosity and delusional optimism in eugenic projects (Kline 2001; Ordover 2003; Black 2003; McLaren 1990; Barrett and Kurzman 2004; Adams 1990; Gould 1981). I argue that in Alberta, "high" eugenics had less of a purchase on the social imaginary than did the "low" variant.

I use the terminology of "high" and "low" to suggest a distinction between the eugenic passions of an intellectual and political elite with their collective eye fixed on a grand future, and the daily constraints experienced by the less elite supporters of eugenics, at the grassroots in the local chapters of the UFWA. Any set of binaries such as "high" versus "low" eugenics is bound to be permeable around the edges, and in this chapter I will inevitably exaggerate the distinction between "high" and "low" eugenics. I must stress that by positing and discussing the idea of "low" eugenics at a distance from the triumphalist dreams of "high" eugenics, I do not intend to sanitize or to excuse the outcomes of eugenic policies, which in Alberta's case involved more than 2,800 people sterilized, many without their knowledge, let alone their consent. Be it by the low road or the high road, eugenics in Alberta arrived at a place of immoral and unjustifiable bodily interventions on its citizens. My intention here is to complicate the eugenic narrative, not to sanitize eugenic practice.

Alberta's Eugenic Imaginary

Alberta produced no major theorists of eugenics or world leaders in the global movement, and its rhetoric and ideology were largely borrowed.[1] Nonetheless, it produced one of the most deeply rooted and pervasive programs of eugenics in the world. Other scholars have speculated on how this program was able to be sustained over the decades, drawing on ideas about static political cultures and the systemization of practices (Dyck 2013; Grekul, Krahn, and Odynak 2004; Caulfield and Robertson 1996). Here I focus on the deep roots of Alberta eugenics, by looking at how the act came into being.

In complicating the eugenic narrative, I follow the perspective adopted by Mariana Valverde with respect to moral reform in English Canada (Valverde 2008). Like her, I seek to understand how particular practices – in this case, eugenic sterilization – were "fundamentally defined and structured by discursive practices which made sense at the time but which now require some historically informed exegesis" (xi). I am not attempting to produce an intellectual history of eugenics via key ideological writings or hegemonic texts; rather, like Valverde, I focus on texts that are "short, popular and geared to action," such as public speeches, organizational memos and resolutions, and editorials (xii). I pay attention not only to the overt meanings of these texts but also to the analogies, metaphors, examples, and extratextual references that together construct the social imaginary of eugenics.

Sterilization happened, I argue, because the social imaginary of early-twentieth-century Alberta permitted both the construction of social problems and the definition of solutions to these problems in ways that favoured public intrusions into private reproductive lives. These moral and normative aspects of the social imaginary came to the fore in the case of sterilization.

I begin with a short chronological outline of the major events in the sexual sterilization program. I then introduce the major player in this particular telling: the UFWA. I describe the earliest appearances of the concept of "eugenics" in the texts of Alberta women's organizations and how this concept blended together with three other preoccupations of maternalist feminist organizations in the hard years of the 1920s – fears that the number of "feeble-minded" people in the province was increasing; xenophobic concerns about the toll that immigration was taking on the province's resources; and, especially, interest in birth control and contraception. These three concerns provided the context in which the Sexual Sterilization Act seemed logical and reasonable.

I argue that in their advocacy for sterilization, Albertan women were ambivalent about the notion of hereditarianism that lies at the heart of "high" eugenics. They opted for an understanding of sterilization whose purpose was not only to "breed out" undesirable characteristics but also to act as a form of protection. Eugenic sterilization could protect society from the "unfit," but it could also protect the "unfit" from the rest of society. These protective claims put forward by advocates of sterilization give the history of eugenics in Alberta a powerfully gendered history, which becomes clear when we look at eugenics as a form of prophylaxis, untangling who was doing the protecting, who needed to be protected, and why.

Eugenic Sterilization in Alberta: A Short History

In 1922 the UFWA passed a resolution at its annual meeting calling for the provincial government to pay more attention to eugenics with special attention to sterilization. The following year, the UFWA executive struck a committee to "draft a resolution re the method of handling the increase in mental defectives,"[2] comprised of three women who would go on to become some of the most vocal advocates of sterilization. In January 1924 a resolution was passed at the annual convention stating that "in view of the alarming increase in the mentally deficient, the danger thereof to the population and the cost to the state, that sterilization be compulsory by law as a means of stopping the mentally deficient from reproducing their own kind." The resolution was carried, but the "compulsory by law" stipulation aroused concern, so a committee was struck to draft a slightly less draconian version.

A revised resolution was passed in 1926, which became the basis for the Sexual Sterilization Act. This resolution called for a committee to be known as the Eugenics Board, which would examine cases brought before them by the administrators of institutions for the mentally ill or delinquent, of inmates who might conceivably be released "with safety to themselves and without menace to the public." The board would determine "whether procreation is inadvisable" and instruct sterilizing surgery to be carried out (UFWA minutes of annual convention, January 1926). The minutes of this meeting note that this resolution was carried unanimously, although all other resolutions put forward that day were noted as simply "carried."

This resolution was virtually identical to the Sexual Sterilization Act, which was introduced to the provincial legislature the following year by the health minister, George Hoadley. The resolution did not pass until a year later, after heated debate and political lobbying pro and con. Before it was repealed and repudiated in 1972, 2,822 Albertans would be sterilized under the authority of the Sexual Sterilization Act (McLaren 1990, 159).

Initially, the legislation covered only the sterilization of inmates of mental institutions who were eligible for discharge back to their communities. These institutions included psychiatric hospitals and residential "training schools" for children who had been diagnosed as "mentally defective." Sterilization could be carried out only if all four members of the Eugenics Board concurred and if the patient in question gave his or her consent. If the patient was incapable of informed consent, permission had to be obtained from his or her legal guardian. However, almost no cases brought before the board were ever turned down.

In 1937, however, the act was amended to permit the sterilization of patients even without their consent. Once again, women's organizations were instrumental in pushing for the act to be expanded. The Eugenics Board was empowered to decide whether consent would be sought for a particular individual, and to order sterilizations without consent if they believed consent would not be forthcoming. In 1942, the act was again amended so as to broaden its powers and apply not only to "mental defectives" but also to people with tertiary syphilis, epilepsy, psychotic episodes, and Huntington's chorea. As time went by, the original scope of the act seemed narrow and restrained compared with its later application. Consistent with this continually broadening scope, the number of sterilizations increased over the years, peaking in the 1950s and 1960s, shortly before the act was repealed (Grekul 2008).

Every scholar who has examined eugenic sterilization in Alberta has noted its gendered, raced, and classed bias. Christian (1974) points out that the majority of those sterilized were unemployed and/or unskilled. He also demonstrates that people of non-British heritage were sterilized out of proportion to their share of Alberta's population, so that the weight of sterilization fell most heavily on people of Eastern European descent and on Aboriginal people. Dyck (2013) similarly points out that Eastern European immigrants were targeted in the Alberta program, whereas African Americans were targeted south of the US–Canada border.

Grekul (2008) observes that most of those sterilized were women (58 per cent) and that the bar for sterilization was set lower for women than for men. In effect, a woman who was only slightly off the norm was more likely to be sterilized than a similar man. Deviance from social and medical ideals was evidently less tolerable in women than in men. Men who were sterilized were much more likely than their female peers to have a record of illegal or violent behaviour, while women were more likely to have a personal record, or a family history, of non-normative sexual activity. As a result, "women were sterilized for 'lesser' reasons, or more aptly, for transgressions that more directly relate to appropriate gender role expectations" (ibid.). These gendered outcomes of the Sterilization Act reflected the gendered concerns that drove the lobbying for sterilization as conducted by the UFWA and other agencies. However, as I will describe, the gendering of eugenics went beyond simply the preponderance of women involved in agitating for the Act, and later, being subjected to it.

The United Farm Women of Alberta

The formal provincial policy to sterilize the "unfit" was driven in large measure by women's organizations from Alberta's agricultural grassroots. The most prominent and powerful of these was the United Farm Women of Alberta, the women's branch of the United Farmers of Alberta. The UFWA was a formidable power in its own right; it and similar organizations such as the Women's Institutes, the Women's Christian Temperance Union, and the Imperial Order Daughters of the Empire saw themselves as representing the interests of women, children, and social well-being in Alberta. This led them to advocate for a variety of measures, including dairy pasteurization, improved and accessible health services, prohibition of alcohol, and services for women travelling alone.

The UFWA was founded in 1915 as a women's auxiliary to the UFA, a populist, agrarian farmers' organization that became a political party and was voted into power in 1921. The UFWA functioned independently of the UFA, although it was not permitted to petition the federal or provincial government on any issue without prior approval by the UFA. In practice, however, the UFWA did not simply comply with the UFA's interests; it lobbied and argued alongside the men of the parent body. The organization attracted some of the busiest agitators for women's rights, such as Irene Parlby and Winifred Ross, who worked closely with their counterparts in neighbouring provinces, including Violet McNaughton and Emily Murphy. The UFA needed the support of the UFWA, especially after women obtained the right to vote provincially in 1916. As Rennie (2000, 186) notes, "there were very few UFWA resolutions not supported by the UFA," including resolutions on equal homesteading, marriage and guardianship rights for women, mothers' pensions, and federal suffrage.

The UFWA was highly centralized, with constant communication and streams of literature flowing from the executive down to the locals. This centralization enabled a focus on particular issues, such as the care of the "feeble-minded." Its written materials included discussion questions and copies of recommended readings (including the speeches of UFWA executive members). Nonetheless, the locals seem to have maintained the same spirit of autonomy towards the central executive as the UFWA did towards the UFA. Locals put forward resolutions at annual meetings that directly contradicted positions taken by the executive, and the correspondence between locals and executives suggests a process of questioning, refining, and reformulating policy planks. This refining took place with regard to sterilization, which was debated and discussed at meetings of local branches, with questions or comments forwarded to the executive. A typical example, from the minutes of the Notre Dame UFWA local on 23 November 1927: "Mrs S read ... a paper on the Sexual Sterilization Act, and after some discussion [we] voted in favour of this Act, and the secretary was requested to send a letter expressing our approval of this step [to the executive] and also that one be sent to all our members" (Glenbow M8365–30).

The UFWA is notable in Alberta history not only because it was the most influential organization as a result of its relationship to the ruling party but also because its membership was restricted to women living on farms. Thus, the members of the UFWA were not part of Alberta's small urban elite, nor were they, in the main, part of the even smaller non-urban elite who made their living off sales and services in farms and small towns. UFWA members celebrated themselves as the salt of the earth, the foundation of Alberta's agrarian economy. When it was expedient to do so, UFWA leaders defined themselves against other women's organizations, their sometime allies, which they believed had a more upper-class or elite make-up, such as the Women's Institutes. Thus, the UFWA was not simply a women's organization; it was an organization for a particular, idealized type of woman.

The push for eugenic sterilization came as a wave of successes by women's organizations crashed into a bleak era in the province's history, when farmers and other "average" Albertans were struggling to survive. Alberta women had campaigned for provincial suffrage in the 1910s, and achieved it in 1916, two years before women gained federal suffrage. Another important cause among women's organizations, prohibition, had become provincial law in 1916. Finally, the Dower Act was passed the same year, which secured married women's interest in property owned by the couple in the event of separation or divorce (about which more will be said in chapter 5). All of these developments were direct results of grassroots and legislative campaigns by the same individuals who would emerge as prominent advocates for sterilization.

But these successes were followed by a gradual decline in Alberta's fortunes, and with it a decline in optimism and expectations of a brighter future. As farm women, the UFWA members were at the epicentre of the economic and climate crises that gripped Alberta in the 1920s and 1930s. The most prominent of these crises were droughts, which began even before the Dust Bowl years in the United States. Rightly or wrongly, Alberta's economic problems were blamed on cabals of eastern Canadian business interests that controlled the rail transport system and the prices for agricultural goods.

The women of the UFWA locals experienced these hard times first-hand, especially in southern Alberta. Such conditions were hardly conducive to imagining a race of superhumans produced by winnowing out the weakest, and the eugenic imagination in Alberta remained focused on the miseries of the here-and-now rather than on future vistas. These conditions figured into their understanding of "low" eugenics, of sterilization as primarily a way to mitigate social and economic strain, rather than as a way to breed a super-race.

As mothers, wives, and farmers, UFWA members experienced the stresses of Alberta life in gendered ways. The UFWA both preached and practised maternal feminism, agitating for social change on the basis of women's status as actual and potential mothers (Davin 1978). In this version of western Canadian populism, the figure of the mother was elevated and glorified, not only by the UFWA but also by the women's sections of other agrarian organizations. Motherhood was described as endowing women with the moral status to change the world, status that was denied to men. Mary Ford, the ardent maternal feminist who wrote the "women's column" in the *Grain Growers' Guide*, repeatedly stressed the visionary power of women and, by contrast, the lack of vision on the part of men, who viewed life through a prism of violence and competition:

> Men of course find it difficult to slough off that superiority complex which they have carried around with them for many centuries but the time is past when they can achieve the greatest good for society by continuing to use women as a kind of eternal Ladies Aid. Women are by nature greater co-operators than men. They have learnt how to serve and work with others in a hard school. They have built their homes upon those qualities of love, loyalty and co-operation, if they are wise mothers, they have nourished these qualities in the hearts of their children and they have a great contribution to make ... It is not in the fighting male of the race, it is in woman that we have the future centre of power in civilization [quote from Benjamin Kidd, "The Science of Power] ("The Home" column, *Grain Growers' Guide*, 1 April 1928).

Interestingly, although UFWA members had to be rural residents and almost all of them were engaged in farming, along with their husbands, the UFWA did not stake its claims for social change on the moral power of women as farmers or producers. Instead, they emphasized causes that could be tied to maternity and to women's role in human reproduction. This was often connected to a surprising degree of anti-male animus, especially after the First World War, when UFWA leaders and advocates argued that men had come perilously close to ruining the world and that only the maternal commitment of women could save it.

The UFWA's maternalist causes included pensions for widowed or abandoned mothers, the right of mothers to retain custody of their children after divorce, the expansion of obstetric and midwifery services for rural women, and, most controversially, the legalization of contraception. They clearly saw themselves as bringers of order to a world confronted with chaos around gender and sexuality, rather than as emancipators or liberators.[3] Their advocacy of sterilization followed from this maternalist bent: their politics encompassed not only improving the experience of reproduction for Albertan women but also ensuring that reproduction was not undertaken by those who were unfit to reproduce.

Early Eugenics

The first appearances of the word "eugenics" in the materials of women's organizations are rather surprising. Far from referring to plans to restrict the reproduction of undesirable people, "eugenics" was initially taken to mean what we would now call sex education and marriage counselling. Mary Ford, in typically extravagant prose, introduced the concept to the farm women who read her page in the *Grain Growers' Guide*:

> Eugenics – well born. Three years ago this word was quite unknown, even to people of culture. Today, it is familiar enough. It teaches that the future will someday be the present and to serve it will be to serve no fiction or phantom but a reality as real as the present generation teaches the responsibility of the noblest and most sacred of the professions, which is parenthood, and it makes a sober and dignified appeal to be regarded as a constituent of the religion of the future ... The child which each one of us has been shall be left no longer to grow in blindness as to the meaning of his place among the generations, the debt he owes to the future, as to the necessity of cleanliness of body and soul and the sacredness of what he is taught too often to believe vulgar and vile ... as to the office of parenthood, the clean true fact of birth, growth and reproduction, as to the necessity of self-control and the honorability of practicing it. ("Eugenics – well born," *Grain Growers Guide*, 25 October 1911)

In response to Ford's early articles, one reader wrote in enthusiastically supporting the principles of eugenics, and adding the distinctively gendered twist that would come to justify women's leading role in organizing reproduction: "The position which you take up with regard to eugenics is the only solution of the future betterment of the human race. Men will try to live up to whatever standard women demand" ("The Home," *Grain Growers' Guide*, 1 May 1912).[4]

Others wrote in to Ford expressing their interest in eugenics and requesting more information. One reader wrote in requesting pamphlets on teaching children about sex, pregnancy, and birth: "I am very much interested in this subject as I am a mother and wish to do my full duty by my children in the very best way possible. I am very much interested in the 'Home' page and especially eugenics. I am saving all the articles" (letter from Mrs E.P., *Grain Growers' Guide*, 10 April 1912).

As noted in chapter 2, the concept of "eugenics" also signalled the need for better obstetric and prenatal care, so that babies would be literally "born well." Mary Ford, in the *Grain Growers' Guide*, contended that the real meaning of "eugenics" was "the safeguarding of mothers" (28 February 1912), which in turn meant greater consideration for pregnant and nursing women, expunging the stigma of illegitimacy, and ensuring proper care for women at the time of delivery – themes she expanded on in her column.

Outside the women's media, it was commonly recognized in the early years that eugenics was a body of knowledge and practice specific to women. In particular, eugenics was associated with the conditions in which women gave birth, as well as knowledge of and education about sex. In a 1918 tract on the hardships faced by Alberta settlers, George Richardson claimed that the absence of eugenic thinking was a barrier to European settlement, for women would avoid the rough conditions of maternity on the prairies: "In all communities whose governments claim to be at all up to date, what is called eugenics is receiving more and more attention, but the Canadian government ... would seem to consider that a hundred and sixty acres [the standard land grant to settlers] covers a multitude of omissions in this regard" (1918, 206).

Richardson went on to describe the "terrible stories of hardship and suffering" he had heard from women about giving birth on isolated homesteads, without medical care, and he linked this directly to the dearth of single women for Alberta's men to marry. Maternal care – the material conditions of reproduction – was a strong focus of UFWA advocacy for decades (see chapter 2). That organization lobbied for more trained midwives, more maternity nurses, and lower doctors' fees for maternity cases, in order to lower maternal and infant mortality rates.

In the interwar era, birth in all its aspects both legitimated and energized the UFWA's work. Alberta women authorized themselves to speak because they were mothers and gave birth, and they claimed the social organization of birth as their particular moral terrain. But maternal feminism alone was not enough to set the UFWA on a course for sterilization. Three other concerns – the care of the "feeble-minded," the problem of excess immigration, and especially the demand for voluntary contraception – also inclined the UFWA to seek reproductive answers to social problems.

The UFWA and "Feeble-Mindedness"

The issue of "feeble-mindedness" or mental disability preoccupied UFWA meetings, to the extent that the minute book for the 1929 Annual Meeting records complaints that the subject was taking up too much time at local meetings. In this, the UFWA was no different from community and professional associations across Canada, for a "preoccupation with the feeble-minded swept the country" in the 1910s (McLaren 1990, 40). Within the UFWA as elsewhere, the problem initially was framed as one of inadequate state institutions to house those who could not live with their families, and the lack of medical expertise for diagnosing or preventing "feeble-mindedness"; but as decades wore on and news of eugenics initiatives in other parts of the world spread in Alberta, controlling the reproduction of the "feeble-minded" became more prominent in discussion.

Exactly what constituted "feeble-mindedness" is not always clear, for the term was used as a catch-all for perceived social or psychological deviancy and its applications grew broader as time wore on. In handwritten notes on a program for the 1924 UFWA annual meeting, Louise Dean, a prominent supporter of social welfare causes, jotted down details of the three grades of "mental defective": the imbecile, the idiot, and the moron (Glenbow M8634 26, Louise Johnston fonds). This taxonomy, familiar from other accounts of eugenic projects elsewhere in North America, held that the idiot and the imbecile were incapable of living without constant supervision and were easily identifiable by their physique and behaviour; the third category, the moron, was the most difficult to manage because morons could appear "normal" and functional, especially early in life. The moron, clearly, was the most at risk for illicit and "dysgenic" reproduction, for she was accessible to men in a way that the other two classes were not. Thus, the problem of "feeble-mindedness" was actually the problem of the liminal or marginally "feeble-minded," who were the most likely to produce children because they were most capable, biologically and socially, of sexual relations. The question of what was to be done with or for the "feeble-minded" thus inevitably turned into the question of how to regulate their reproduction.

The first UFWA reference to "feeble-mindedness" occurs in the minutes of the 15 December 1921 meeting of the UFWA executive, at which the need for an expert to address the group on "the increase of the feeble-minded" was raised. Records from these years reveal extensive discussion about the "feeble-minded," and particularly discussion of the toll they were supposedly taking on Alberta's treasury. Descriptions of the tribulations of the "feeble-minded" in the community were interspersed with sunny and undoubtedly sanitized accounts of visits to the modern, "scientific" psychiatric hospitals at Ponoka and Red Deer, in which the "feeble-minded" could live permanently or intermittently, in peace and without disturbance to the community.

As the decades wore on, this broad concern about the well-being of "feeble-minded" people coalesced into a discussion of three options for dealing with them: segregation in institutions; restriction by laws limiting what they were allowed to do in the community, particularly through laws restricting marriage; and sterilization. The latter option emerged as the most popular, for it was perceived as addressing not only the immediate problem of "feeble-minded" people being both victims and victimizers of the "normal," but also the possibility of a future in which the "feeble-minded" outnumbered the rest of the population. At the 1924 UFWA convention, Irene Parlby argued in favour of sterilization over other options, on the grounds that women should be concerned about what she called the "brutal ratio" in which the "feeble-minded" out-reproduced the rest of the population. She then laid out the three alternatives and concluded that "women, as mothers of the race, [should] take a sympathetic and intelligent interest in this problem" ("UFWA in Annual Convention," *The UFA*, 26 February 1924).

The UFWA and Immigration

The UFWA's concerns about the "feeble-minded" in Alberta were inextricably tied to their nativism and xenophobia concerning immigrants. This preoccupation was shared by most of civil society in Alberta and the rest of Canada. UFWA presidents and leading lights, including the long-serving president Irene Parlby and her comrades in activism Nellie McClung and Emily Murphy, were preoccupied with the problems supposedly being generated by excess immigration.

The link between "feeble-mindedness" and immigration was made through the assumption that immigrants who did not come from the British Isles were more likely than those born in Canada or in the British Isles to be "mentally defective." In Alberta, most of the anti-immigrant animus was focused on immigrants from Central and Eastern Europe, who were arriving in the West by the thousands, having been brought in by the federal interior minister, Clifford Sifton, whose goal was to fill up the prairies with people who were accustomed to harsh weather and intense agrarian labour. White Anglo-Saxon Protestant Albertans shared the belief that the federal government was too lax in screening potential immigrants and that it was filling the West's vacant spaces without regard for the impact on the people already living there.

Immigrants from Eastern Europe tended to have higher birth rates, at least initially, than Anglo-Canadians, and this led to fears that British stock would be swamped. According to Corbett (1979, 130), in 1926, 37 per cent of all recorded births were to Canadian-born women; 19 per cent to British-born; and 44 per cent to "foreign"-born (i.e., born neither in Canada nor in Britain). Maude Riley, founder of the Alberta Council on Child Welfare, expressed these fears of engulfment by "inferior" classes of people:

> I say Canada is a vast country rolling in the wealth of her natural resources and her fertile plains. But who are going to develop these – true Canadians? Or in twenty five years is she going to be ruled and dominated by those who do not or perhaps those who will not appreciate or understand our Canadian ideals and customs. Ponder this question for there is none more vital to our beloved dominion ... We [have] spent vast sums of money in bringing foreigners to this country and now contemplate spending other vast sums to rectify this mistake. (undated speech, probably 1928, Glenbow M8401, file 28 – Maude Riley fonds)

It was at the 1924 annual convention – the same one at which the first resolution on sterilization was passed – that the UFWA first linked immigration to "feeble-mindedness," in a resolution from the UFWA committee on legislation. The resolution began: "Whereas it is vital to the best interests of Canadian citizenship that steps be taken to check the

flow of the mentally weak and degenerate immigration from Europe."
It then called for all potential immigrants to be examined by a psychia-
trist at their point of embarkation.

This link between immigration and "feeble-mindedness" was
strengthened at the 1926 convention, when a delegate from Waskatenau,
in a speech supporting sexual sterilization, diverged from her remarks
to link eugenics with immigration. Sterilization alone would not lift the
burden of "feeble-mindedness," as long as deficient immigrants continued to come in:

> Digressing from the resolution a moment, we would do well to keep clear-
> ly before us the percentage of mental defectives in Alberta who are not of
> Canadian stock. The figures are positively startling. Of the 140 patients in
> the provincial training schools, 24% were of native Canadian [born in
> Canada, not aboriginal] stock, 29% were from the British Isles, 16% were
> from the US and 31% were from central Europe and other countries. These
> figures should spur us to demand once again that the federal immigration
> authorities exercise the very strictest care in examining the mental fitness
> of every immigrant entering Canada. It is not too much to demand that
> immigrants should furnish sworn records of the mental health of their
> forebears. No immigrant can be called an asset who is likely to become an
> inmate of a public institution maintained at the expense of the people of
> Alberta. (preamble to resolution from Waskatenau local branch of UFWA,
> PAA 1971.420, file 33)

The most often cited support for the link between Eastern European
origin and "feeble-mindedness" was a survey of Alberta carried out
by the Canadian National Committee on Mental Hygiene, an Ontario-
based group. In this survey, published in 1921, alarmingly high rates of
sexual immorality and social disorder were found to prevail in Alberta,
linked to the number of recent Slavic immigrants. The notion that this
might be due to social dislocation and the economic stress involved in
establishing oneself in a new country was not entertained. As McLaren
(1990, 99) notes, the Committee on Mental Hygiene, "unable to empa-
thize with the plight of strangers in a strange land, put down as evidence of mental slowness the confusion of new arrivals."

While Eastern European immigrants faced the bulk of criticism, some
also accused the otherwise sacrosanct United Kingdom of "dumping"
its unemployables by encouraging them to immigrate to Canada. This
criticism was pronounced after the First World War, which had resulted

a "surplus" of women (i.e., their prospective husbands had been killed). Federal immigration authorities encouraged these women to come to Canada, yet at the provincial level, Alberta elites complained about the low quality of the girls who were answering "Canada's call to women" (so it was phrased in advertisements for the White Star Line, which transported thousands of immigrants).

The UFWA and Birth Control

Sterilization of the "feeble-minded" was also linked to advocacy for (voluntary) birth control. It is worth noting that at the same time that the UFWA and others were agitating for eugenic sterilization of the "unfit," women who actually wanted to stop childbearing or to limit the number of children they bore were legally prohibited from getting the information they needed in order to do so. Within the debates of women's organizations, voluntary birth control was actually more controversial than sterilization of the "feeble-minded," because it appeared to make non-marital sex more accessible and appealing, and because it might encourage the abandonment of women's sacred duty to reproduce the population.

Birth control was controversial; even so, the UFWA and others sought repeal of the laws that had criminalized the dissemination of information about family planning. They did so, however, in terms that linked voluntary birth control and sterilization as two facets of the same goal: rationalized, planned reproduction.

Many women would have heard of the case of Georgina Sackville, a Calgary woman and superintendent of a home for unmarried mothers, who offered a pamphlet on birth control for sale and was threatened by the post office with the loss of her postal privileges if she attempted to send such "objectionable circulars" through the mail (letter from postal superintendent J.B. Corley, 27 September 1929, Glenbow MS 6549).

An official history of the UFWA, written in 1930, also linked sterilization with birth control, perceiving these as two fronts in the same struggle against irresponsible reproduction. Beginning in the early 1920s, the anonymous historian wrote, "agitation began for birth control information and sterilization of the unfit. [This agitation] ... has since borne fruit in a demand for clinics where contraceptive advice may be obtained and in the Sterilization Act" (*History of the United Farm Women of Alberta*, 7, Glenbow M1749, file 45). On the surface, this linkage may seem odd, given that the Sexual Sterilization Act imposed strong pressures to be sterilized, by withholding freedom if institutional inmates did not consent, while the establishment of birth control clinics suggests a free flow of information and uncoerced decision-making. For many maternal feminists of the time, however, eugenic sterilization and voluntary birth control were two sides of the same coin.

Both social projects were understood as manifestations of the same progressive urge to bring human reproduction under scientific control. With the advance of such rationalized reproduction, childbearing would become part of a conscious social calculus along utilitarian lines: What reproductive practices would provide the greatest good for the greatest number? The notion of an individual right to reproduce or not reproduce, or of entitlement to all possible options for reproduction, was absent. Its place was filled by the idea of collective moral responsibility on the part of women to ensure that reproduction favoured the overall well-being of Alberta. Access to voluntary birth control was desirable insofar as it would alleviate the same problems that eugenic sterilization was intended to alleviate – the production of children by women who, for various reasons, ought not to be producing them.

At the 1933 annual meetings of the UFWA,

> Dr Mildred Newell spoke on the subject of family limitation, which she said the medical profession regarded as the urgent need of the times, She made a strong appeal for a contraceptive clinic in this province whose objects would be to prevent the procreation of the physically and mentally unfit, to do away with the ghastly business of abortion, and to alleviate the suffering of the mother overburdened with children. A big step in this direction was taken in 1925 when the province of Alberta began to work on the sterilization of the mentally unfit. ("Thursday's sessions," *The UFA*, 1 February 1933)

Dr Newell went on to speak of the importance of birth control as a form of progress and enlightenment in that it brought voluntary parenthood within the control of individual women. However, the examples she used to illustrate her case make it clear that she was not imagining an empowered, modern woman making use of birth control to optimize her life, but "bad" reproducers who ought to be stopped:

> Perhaps you would be interested in a few of the cases which have been under observations for some years in connection with the provincial baby clinic in Edmonton. In one case the woman was 27, the oldest boy nine

years old, and there are eight children including one pair of twins. The mother is in pretty poor condition, very nervous, and expects to be confined in March ... Things are too much for her and she feels that she is unable to carry on and is asking for "something to be done." In my opinion, that something should have been done three or four years ago. ("Birth control, address presented by Dr Folinsbee Newell at the 19th annual convention," PAA 1971.420)

In 1937, ten years after the Sexual Sterilization Act was passed, the Alberta Family and Child Welfare Council, a body with strong input from women's organizations, called for birth control clinics to be set up in the cities using exactly the same images and examples of "cases" that had been employed to argue for sterilization:

When you visit a family and see the mother having a baby every ten or twelve months, see her ruining her health and endangering her life, when you see the children neglected and under-nourished and ill-clothed, then you realize that charity means more than distributing a few clothes and hampers. I believe we must in the name of Christianity help these families to limit their families to a number that they can safely bear, adequately support, and care for ... Typical cases chosen at random: Case 1: mother 24 years 8 children. On relief, Husband unemployed for several years. Mother extremely frail. Case 2. 13 children. On relief. Eldest girl in sanatorium with TB. Case 3. Three children. On relief, all children suffering from congenital prosis or hereditary paralysis of the eyelids. Two almost blind. Case 4. Three children. Living in utterly miserable basement rooms. On relief. Five year old idiot, two year old idiot unable to lift head or show signs of intelligence. New baby. Two year old idiot died May 1938. (untitled newspaper clipping from *Calgary Herald*, 26 November 1938, M6958, Maude Riley fonds)

Ambivalence about Hereditarianism

These images of reproductive misery evoked by both sterilization and birth control characterize what I am calling "low" eugenics, as distinct from "high." "High" eugenics – the project of creating a new and improved human race – is founded on a belief in hereditarianism, that is, the idea that many traits, both desirable and undesirable, are passed from one generation to the next through sexual reproduction. According to this belief, if the portion of the population that reproduces consists primarily of people with desirable traits, over the course of a few generations those traits will come to predominate in a population, raising its quality. Deliberately manipulating the composition of the segment of the population that reproduces is a way to gradually improve population quality, even though the full flowering of the "master race" may only occur in a utopian future a few generations away. In practice, this triumphalist eugenics focused on removing such supposedly inheritable traits as "mental defect," criminality, promiscuity, and neurological conditions such as epilepsy and schizophrenia by sterilizing those who bore those traits.

Alberta had its share of triumphalist voices heralding the arrival of utopia through eugenics. The UFA, as a populist organization and as a provincial government, leaned towards a millennial view of peace and prosperity through agrarian cooperation, and eugenics fit into this view, as in this rather overheated broadside from the secretary of the Queenstown Board of Trade. In describing how "from among the weeds and outhouses of a worn-out system of competition are rising the slender towers of the wonderful structure of the future" would arise, he claimed that "wars will be unknown, class dissensions forever over; race lines broken down, hates and jealousies past. The human race will make eugenics assist evolution and a race of super-men will continue the work of co-operation that we are just beginning" ("The wheat pool and the new age," *The UFA*, 1 September 1927, 9).

The influential Maude Riley, chair of the Calgary Local Council of Women, made the same point in 1923 with slightly less hyperbole: "We cannot have progressive civilization until the more richly endowed are given the opportunity and encouragement to reproduce their kind in greater numbers and the mentally deficient prevented" (report from Law Committee of the UFWA, Glenbow M8401–51).

However, hereditarian logic did not have a firm foothold in Alberta. While some supported these biologically bound arguments, others doubted whether hereditarianism would contribute to racial betterment. Early in the century, the superintendent of neglected children took an explicitly anti-hereditarian stance, perhaps in order to ward off criticism that spending money on the children of "defectives" was pointless. He described five boys who had been removed from the care of "unfit" parents in Red Deer:

[From] homes which would have been a disgrace to the most decadent race of the east, these five sturdy and promising youngsters ... have been transformed from pitiable wrecks of humanity into bright ambitious lads, the stuff of which virile men are made ... Two years ago the five boys were physically unfit throughout a long course of neglect and malnutrition from which spring physical and mental enfeeblement and a process had begun which, if it had not been stayed, would doubtless have led to the boys' enlistment in that army of undesirables which threats in decadent communities to sap the very foundations of society ... [One boy] to the untrained eye appeared quite a hopeless specimen of the genus homo, and with a gift for getting himself into trouble and not of the lighter sort, he would have been despaired of by many an expert in eugenics ... Today the abnormal tendencies have been eradicated and the street urchin has been transformed into a normally constituted boy and is doing well. ("Work accomplished by superintendent," *Edmonton Capital*, 10 June 1911)

A contemporary article in the liberal *Western Globe* expressed similar doubts about hereditarian determinism and argued for the improvement of living conditions as the best way to improve the quality of the population:

Eugenics is the science of racial improvement by application of the laws of heredity, namely by encouraging the survival and propagation of the fittest in all classes of society and by seeking to cut off the lines of inheritance of the unfit in all classes of society. We do not however know enough about human genetics to predict always the fittest and the unfittest. Some of the greatest men the world has ever seen have sprung from humble stocks. Eugenics therefore should aim at giving every individual that is worth preserving in every class the chance of survival. A living wage enough to ensure a sanitary dwelling and a sufficiency of nourishing food for parents and family should be possible for every labourer and artisan. ("How insanity is increasing," *Western Globe*, 16 August 1912)

Through the 1920s, as eugenic "science" developed in the United States and Europe, Albertans were well aware that scientific opinion was tilting towards hereditarianism. Newspapers of the day carried articles about international eugenics events, particularly the Second International Eugenics Conference in 1921, and quoted the views of American eugenics advocates such as Charles Davenport, the founder of the American Eugenics Record Office at Cold Spring Harbor, and

G. Stanley Hall, president of the American Psychological Association. But even during the 1920s, Albertans were expressing doubts about the heritability of mental defects and whether sterilization would prevent them in the next generation. In the program of the 1927 Calgary Baby Welfare Week, organized by the local Council of Women, a psychology professor at the University of Toronto suggested that

> original estimates of the percentage of mental defect due to inheritance were too high. Instead of 85% ... a closer approximation is probably 50% ... The value of sterilization as a preventive agency must be seriously questioned. In fact ... sterilization, even if universally adopted and vigourously prosecuted, would materially reduce the amount of mental defect ... and my considered opinion is that it should not be adopted, as yet at any rate, as a provincial policy. (Glenbow 8401–30)

The same program contained several other anonymous articles arguing that "mental defectives" were not a menace to the rest of the population and that most could be trained to become useful citizens. In a similar vein, the provincial public health minister, in his message to the UFWA annual convention in 1926, estimated that one out of every five children born to a "defective" parent were themselves defective, a much lower rate than found in eugenic opinion elsewhere (Glenbow M1749–44, minutes of 1926 Annual Convention).

But even if many Albertans were sceptical about hereditarianism, they still found reasons to support the sterilization of the "unfit." Eugenic, hereditarian sterilization might be dubious, but opinion leaders made a case for sterilization on "euthenical" grounds. The term "euthenics" – as distinct from eugenics – referred to the quality of childrearing. The presumed inability of the "feeble-minded" to raise their children properly was thus seen as a euthenical problem, the implication being that more and more children would end up as charges on the cash-strapped province and its municipalities:

> Even admitting that some of the offspring of the mentally defective parents may be of normal mentality at birth, yet it is an accepted fact that it is impossible for these parents, *especially if the mother is the defective*, to train and develop the characters of these children so they will become decent adult citizens. Almost invariably they become enlisted in the ranks of criminal classes. Dr. Hincks, chairman of the Canadian Council of Mental Hygiene, not long ago said "I find myself favouring sterilization not on

eugenical grounds alone but also on euthenical as well. I have been struck by the fact that feeble minded *mothers* are notoriously incapable of bringing up their children and I am convinced they should not be given the opportunity to thwart and stifle healthy child development. Sterilization would prevent them from having the responsibility of child care." (Report of the Convenor of Health, UFWA Annual Convention 1927, Glenbow M1749–44; emphasis added)

In a similar vein, an anonymous writer for the program of Calgary's Baby Welfare Week in 1936, discussing the possibility of providing training for people of limited mental ability, stated that even in the absence of a biological basis for "feeble-mindedness," the reproductive and domestic behaviour of this population was a threat: "Morons tend to marry morons and without any provision or forethought for the future, without the ability to maintain and train children, they produce families almost double the average in numbers, many of whom will have to be maintained by the state, whilst the other stocks are dwindling" (Glenbow M8401, file 35).

This euthenic argument for sterilization was more profoundly gendered than the hereditarian argument. If we look only at the results of this policy, in the form of the thousands of Albertans who were sterilized, it does not matter much whether sterilization was motivated by hereditarian or by euthenical arguments, as both arguments led to the same end: legalized (and in some cases forced) sterilization of the allegedly unfit. But from a gender-analytic perspective, these arguments are very distinct.

The hereditarian argument attached itself equally to men and women, as both parents were assumed to be bearers of the deficient "germ plasm" that produced more genetic defects in the next generation. In contrast, the euthenical argument was about women and mothering, not men and parenting. It followed that women who could not be good mothers, producing high-quality children, should not be mothers at all. The euthenical argument also served to distinguish "low" from "high" eugenics, as euthenics did not presume that error could be "bred out" of the race, producing a more nearly perfect population. If sterilization is understood as a pre-emptive response to the spectre of ineffective mothering, not just the consequence of a belief that some biological material is inherently defective, the passionate commitment to sterilization among maternalist feminist organizations like the UFWA becomes even clearer.

Sterilization and Protection

When Mrs Jean Field, UFWA vice-president and a founding member of the Eugenics Board, addressed the UFWA's 1932 annual meeting on the subject of eugenic sterilization, she did not offer "high" eugenic visions of humanity's evolution towards a greater race. Instead of triumphalist rhetoric, her address consisted of a catalogue of human misery, supposedly cases of people who had been sterilized and whose lives were to some degree relieved by the operation. One patient was described as

> an intelligent, rather capable woman. Husband is a moron, there are nine children and three children died soon after birth. Of six living children, three are low grade defectives, probably idiot; two are borderline defectives and one is of normal intelligence but very nervous. The mother married at 16 and is now only 35. (PAA PR 1971.420, file 19)

Another patient was a

> man of 40, history of nervousness and leanings towards religious fanaticism. Father alcoholic, brother insane. Wife is a thin wisp of a woman worn out with childbearing. There have been twelve children, one died at thirteen months, one died at the training school. Of the 10 living children, two are feeble-minded and blind, one is epileptic, two more are borderline defectives and are malnourished, five are normal so far. (ibid.)

Mrs Field went on to praise the sterilization program, but she did not frame it as a way to purify and concentrate the best "stock" in a population. Instead, she described sterilization as a form of charity. It relieved the "feeble-minded" populace and their families of the "burden" of uncontrolled reproduction, and it provided a safe and arguably humane alternative to shutting up the potentially reproductive "feeble-minded" in institutions.

> The sterilization act brought into being a new phase of health work which will be of great benefit to ... Alberta. Do not misunderstand me. It is not a cure all. There will always be the need of segregation in institutions of large numbers of people. But it is one of many sane, practical and humane measures which must be adopted to relieve in a slight degree the appalling problems of the mentally incompetent. (ibid.)

Mrs Field's portrayal of sterilization exemplified the way in which the UFWA and others organized their support for sterilization around the idea of protection – both protection *of* the "feeble-minded" from predatory others, and protection of society *from* the "feeble-minded." The latter interpretation of protection – the idea that society must be saved from the "inferior" – has received the most attention in the historiography of eugenics, possibly because it tied in most clearly with overt racism and produced lurid doomsday scenarios of what would happen to "normal" society if the "feeble-minded" were not stopped. Protecting society from the "feeble-minded" led most notoriously to eugenic exterminations in Nazi Germany during the 1930s and 1940s.

However, the idea of sterilization as a protective measure *for* the "feeble-minded" was also an important component of pro-sterilization arguments in Alberta. Protecting the "feeble-minded" – often equated with children's vulnerability to predators – was consistent with the maternal feminist ethic of care for the weaker.

It is difficult to say how much of this professed concern for the vulnerabilities of those with mental disabilities was genuine, and how much was simply an acceptable maternal facade for a desire to eliminate the "inferior." That said, Albertan sterilization advocates, especially women's organizations, were strongly aware that being mentally challenged in early-twentieth-century Alberta was a dangerous state, one that left women in particular vulnerable to exploitation. Unwanted reproduction was only one of the ways in which vulnerable women could be victimized, and perhaps not even the most damaging one, but it was one for which the UFWA and others thought they could find a solution.

Advocates for sterilization stressed the importance of rallying public support by arousing sympathy for the "feeble-minded," as well as awareness of the threat they posed to the wider society. For instance, Evelyn Carson, a prominent supporter of sterilization from the Calgary Local Council of Women, urged her fellow member to be "more [vocal] about public sympathy with the feebleminded and a scientific understanding of their needs. Miss Carson urged the need for sterilization of the unfit and quoted many noted doctors who favoured this means of protecting such persons" (Glenbow. file M8541-24, Minutes of Calgary Local Council of women, 21 January 1921).

Irene Parlby, first president of the UFWA and first female cabinet minister in Alberta, also framed sterilization as a means to protect the "feeble-minded" from a cruel world: "The danger[] in letting the high grade defective remain at large [is] not, as one doctor put it, that they are not fit for the community *but that the community is not fit for them*. There are too many bad people in the community ready to take advantage of the weaknesses of these poor defectives and use them for their own evil ends" ("Mental deficiency: an address delivered by the Hon Mrs Parlby before the UFWA January 1924," PAA 1971.420; emphasis added). Sterilization would protect the "feeble-minded" not only from their own limitations and vulnerabilities but also from what Parlby saw as the harsher, less humane alternatives of permanent segregation or prohibition of marriage. These two alternatives imposed too much suffering on the "feeble-minded" and their families: "Some parents might be thankful to have the nervous strain of caring for a poor idiot child removed from the home, but they might very strenuously object to the removal of a child who was a high grade defective" (ibid.). With sterilization, the "high grade defective" could remain in the home, and possibly even marry: Parlby and others saw this as superior to an unhappy life in an institution (see also McLaren 1990, 98).

Parlby's remarks, in the run-up to the passage of the Sexual Sterilization Act, drew on a long history of expressed concern about the vulnerabilities of the "feeble-minded." Provincial bodies tasked with protection of the weak and needy, especially the Provincial Superintendent of Neglected and Delinquent Children – an important ally of women's groups – argued that the "feeble-minded" were in danger, besides being potentially dangerous:

Almost every day the mail brings us one or more heart-rending appeals from parents who have one or more mentally defective children in their homes asking that some step be taken to protect them from themselves ... We have invariably to reply that no provision has been made for this class and under these circumstances the department can do absolutely nothing ... Society owes it to the mentally defective boys and girls to save them from themselves and make their lives as happy and useful as possible. Lacking in self-control, many of them are incapable of resisting temptation, their wills are weak, they act upon impulse rather than reason, are easily led and susceptible to criminal influence and designing person and fall into criminal ways and sooner or later are branded criminals and herded with others of that ilk. (1914 Annual Report of Superintendent of Neglected Children 1914, Medicine Hat Archives, Baldwin Reichwein fonds. M 2008.1)

By 1918, the superintendent reported that it was becoming

> increasingly apparent that the mental defective problem will not be per-
> manently solved until we have some adequate means of caring for mental
> defectives of child-bearing age. With the impulses and passions of adults
> and the minds of children, these unfortunates become the victims of de-
> signing and vicious individuals. (1918 Annual Report of Superintendent
> of Neglected Children, Medicine Hat Archives, Baldwin Reichwein fonds,
> M 2008.1)

While official pronouncements spoke of "defectives" and "unfortu-
nates" of "child-bearing age," other sources make it clear the main problem was not adults generally, it was women specifically. The notion that
the "feeble-minded" needed the protection of sterilization was drawn
from observations of young women who appeared to be reproducing
against their will, or at the very least against their own better interests.

The convenor of child welfare for the UFWA, in her 1926 address to
the annual convention, strongly advocated sterilization as benefiting
both the "feeble-minded" and Alberta as a whole. The examples she
used were not of parents who passed down their problems to their offspring, or of hereditary illnesses transmitted across generations, but of
women who gave birth outside the framework of marriage:

> In one of our institutions we have a young woman of 21 with the mentality
> of a girl of nine years. She is the mother of three illegitimate children ... At
> Ponoka [the provincial psychiatric hospital], patients are quite often able
> to be sent home, having improved sufficiently to be quite harmless and
> able to attend to their work in the house or on the farm. In the course of
> time, more children are born. I have been told of one case of a woman who
> was allowed to go home for a year or two on three different occasions.
> Each time a baby was born before she came back. 3,700 children in this
> province have one parent in the Ponoka hospital. (Minute Book of UFWA
> Annual Convention 1926, Glenbow M1749)

This view that sterilization (of women) would benefit those sterilized
was expressed by Alberta women's rights activist Nellie McClung in
her memoirs, published in 1945. In that book, McClung described the
case of "Katie," a "slow" teenager who was starting to attract attention
from boys. Her mother sought out sterilization for her out of concern

for what might happen; her father objected (significantly, he was explicitly described as an immigrant not born in Canada). The maternal protective drive of Katie's mother eventually prevailed, Katie was sterilized, and on McClung's next visit, Katie was properly domesticated rather than sexualized – at home knitting a Norwegian sweater rather than hanging around with boys. Her parents were happy and relieved. How exactly sterilization was supposed to incline Katie towards knitting rather than sex is not entirely clear, but the message is plain: sterilization had saved Katie (and her parents) from tragedies they were not equipped to handle (McClung 1945).

These concerns about the problems of "feeble-minded" girls being "taken advantage of" and having babies had not been invented by sterilization advocates for propaganda purposes. The case files of the provincial attorney general tasked with enforcing the Children of Unmarried Parents Act contain frequent references to "feeble-minded" girls being "used" and impregnated by peers and older men. Expressions of concern emanated from local authorities to the provincial authorities, as in a letter from the municipal secretary of Forty Mile District, who wrote about a teenage girl in his jurisdiction who "has recently been sent to Calgary as she is about to become a mother. She has been placed in the care of the Salvation Army ... The girl is feeble minded and unless she is placed in an institution where she will be protected this trouble may occur again. Will you kindly look into the matter and advise?" (PAA, file 75.126 3342a, box 174).

While "this trouble" was never explicitly named as rape or sexual assault, the more detailed case files make it clear that this was what investigators and community members believed was happening. Although mentions of such crimes proliferated in the files of the Attorney General and the Superintendent of Neglected Children, prosecutions almost never succeeded. In the few cases where prosecution was not abandoned, the case was usually settled by a one-time cash payment from the accused men to the father of the pregnant woman, in exchange for the case being dropped without admission of either wrongdoing or paternity.

The case of Edith J, a pregnant teenager, is typical and so is worth drawing out at length. A complaint was made by her stepfather. Several different local men had been identified as possible the possible father, and the stepfather wanted child support payments. The case was referred from the Superintendent of Neglected Children to the Attorney General with the notation that this case is a very sad one as the girl concerned is decidedly a mental defective and in my opinion a great wrong has been done. It is out of the question to proceed further in the matter under the CUPA as it would be impossible to prove just who is the father of the child. I am of the opinion that a criminal charge should be laid against these men as an outrage has definitely been perpetrated on this poor girl. (letter from KC McLeod to Charles Becker, 2 September 1925, PAA, file 75.126 3342a, box 174)

Edith was tested by a psychologist from the University of Alberta, who found her to be of subnormal intelligence. Her stepfather testified that

I am the stepfather of Edith J ... She was 18 last June. Edith is feeble minded at all times. At some times she is worse than others. She is very slow at thinking and counting. She talks very vulgarly at times. She has been worse since she had double pneumonia three years ago. Jack A. has known her about two years. He lives about a mile and a half away from us. He has been over three or four times to our place. He has never been out with her as far as I know ... She has known Willie S. for about nine years. We live two miles from where S. was brought up. He was over here several times a year for the last six years. She has known Julius S. for about one year. He was never at our place that I know of and I don't know much about him. Edith was working at Peter W.'s [house] when the trouble occurred. We always kept her at home as much as possible. She worked out at three other places for a short time but the above are the only occasions when she has been away. ("Crime report of unlawful carnal knowledge," 18 September 1925, PAA, file 75.126 3342a, box 174)

"Keeping Edith at home" did not protect her from the predations of local men. Investigators brought in four men named above for questioning, each of whom implicated the others in the pregnancy. The investigators believed that all four men had had sex with Edith, who was reported to have "the mind of an eight-year-old child" (ibid.).

The case was eventually abandoned because it was impossible to establish who among the four men "present at the same time" Edith was assaulted had actually had sex with her. Nonetheless, the community's feelings were roused against the men, who were thought to have taken advantage of a disabled girl, as the superintendent noted in a letter to the Attorney General protesting the decision to drop the case: "For your information, there appears to be a great deal of unrest in the district of B. at the apparent inactivity of government official in this case" (letter from McLeod to Becker, 26 November 1925, PAA, file 75.126 3342a, box 174).

For all the Edith J's in the province, justice might better have been served by effective prosecution for sexual assault or, even more fundamentally, by the transformation of gender regimes that accorded power and apparent impunity to men. But in the absence of either of those changes to Alberta society, sterilization seemed a way to at least mitigate, if not set right, the vulnerability of such women.

However, the push for sterilization was not animated primarily by altruistic concern for the well-being of young women like Edith J. If the "feeble-minded" needed protection, so did the collective entity called "Alberta society." In Alberta, hereditarianism was not universally accepted as truth, and the "high" eugenic vision of racial triumphalism was more muted than elsewhere Canada. When the province's sterilization advocates arrived at a consensus, the focus was on the nature of the threat posed by the "feeble-minded": they and their offspring were an economic drain on the province, eating up money, welfare, and state resources. In the 1926 program for Calgary's Baby Welfare Week, an article on "mental hygiene" contended that

> it costs the country millions of dollars annually to keep [the feeble-minded] in the community and yet we go on allowing them to keep propagating their kind to be an added burden for future generations. For the low grade defectives, institutional care and sterilization seem to be the only measures that will decrease the problem that is today piling up a tremendous debt against us financially, physically and morally. (Glenbow M8401, file 35)

During the 1920s, a time of economic peril and uncertainty, many different groups were staking claims on the government's limited financial resources, including veterans of the Great War, the unemployed, and abandoned mothers (see chapter 5). The spectre of "feeble-minded" parents drawing off state resources and money through their ineffective care of their offspring was often invoked by sterilization advocates to buttress the argument that these people had no business becoming parents in the first place.

In resolutions at annual meetings, UFWA speakers argued that the mentally deficient were unaffordable. A speaker from the Waskatenau local branch, in her preamble to yet another resolution calling for sterilization, pointed out that the number of "mentally defective" people in Alberta had increased from 251 in 1922 to 657 in 1925 and that each of these people, when institutionalized, cost Alberta taxpayers an average of 76 cents per day. The public, furthermore, was unaware of the threat posed by this group: "Public opinion at present is ignorant of the danger of the increase of the feeble-minded. Public opinion must be educated and aroused" (PAA 1971.420, file 33, preamble to resolution from Waskatenau local). The speaker proposed that sterilization first be imposed on people convicted of offences against children who were found to be "feeble-minded." The public would then grow used to the idea of sterilization and link it to protection of Alberta's most valuable resources:

> There must be a starting point for the radical treatment of the mentally defective and why not start upon such persons who bring themselves within the law by committing crimes the very nature of which show the offenders not only to be mentally defective but also a danger to society? ... Perhaps public opinion would more easily be awakened and educated to demand and support a measure that would punish offenders against children ... This resolution suggests a measure of sterilization in the hope that it may prove the thin edge of the wedge.

The public resistance to sterilization that the Waskatenau speaker alluded to was also found within the UFWA. Some objected to sterilization on religious grounds, because it took away the God-given ability to be fruitful, and others on ethical grounds, because it involved the medical modification of a healthy body. No one, however, seems to have objected on the grounds that involuntary sterilization was an affront to human rights and personal integrity. This view of sexual sterilization had to wait several decades to gain purchase in Alberta.

Although the UFWA as a whole led the drive for sterilization legislation, some individuals and local branches demurred on the grounds that sterilization was unnatural and too invasive and that it would not adequately protect the sterilized person from predation. Interestingly, the same arguments used to support sterilization – that it was necessary to protect "feeble-minded" women from the worst consequences of predation by men – were now turned against it, with the notion that sterilization would not be enough to protect these women and would only gloss over the problem. The Camrose local put forward an unsuccessful resolution at the 1926 annual meeting calling for the UFWA to oppose sterilization on the grounds that it "constitutes a violent and drastic invasion ... and does not take away the sexual desire, and still leaves the patient utterly lacking in moral resistance and leaving them prey to the dangers of social contact with people of low moral standards" (*The UFA*, 16 January 1926).

In invoking the figure of a sterilized person fallen "prey" to those of "low moral standards," the members of the Camrose local undoubtedly had women in mind. "Feeble-minded" women could become prey to rapacious men, but nowhere in the discourse around sterilization was the figure of a man as a sexual victim invoked. In this way, as in so many others, the rhetoric of eugenics, sterilization, and reproduction was profoundly gendered.

Conclusion

After the passage of the Sexual Sterilization Act, eugenics largely dropped off the radar of women's organizations in Alberta. Alcohol and drugs came to the forefront as the social concern that the "mothers of the race" needed to address to protect the future. When sterilization did merit a mention, it was in one of two contexts: self-congratulation on passing such a progressive and useful law, or calls for even more stringent measures to prevent the "feeble-minded" from procreating. In 1937, the Alberta Federation of Women, a new umbrella body, called on the government (which was no longer a UFA government, the disasters of the Depression having forced it from office) to include "compulsory sterilization of problem cases and patients outside institutions." While not willing to go that far, the new Social Credit government did pass changes to the act that had the effect of reducing the need to obtain consent on behalf of those being sterilized (Minutes of Alberta Federation of Women Executive, 23 September 1937, Glenbow M-8401-7).

The sexual sterilization project in Alberta was gendered in many ways, beyond the obvious reality that it was a project driven by women. Because sterilization had to do with pregnancy and children (or the prevention of same), within the social imaginary of Alberta at the time it defaulted to women, for reproductive politics were understood to be the moral property of women. Maternal feminism, the notion that it was up to women to right the wrongs of society and protect the vulnerable, made for a natural match between the UFWA and the idea of sexual sterilization. "The vulnerable" might be construed as "feeble-minded" people at risk of disastrous reproduction, or as Alberta society, itself at risk of disastrous reproduction and its social and economic costs. Whichever construction was chosen, the idea of eugenics as protection from harm animated the movement in Alberta and distinguished it as a primarily "low" rather than "high" eugenic undertaking.

In addition, "eugenics," the broader social project within which sterilization was eventually incorporated, had already been staked out as an area of gendered concern in the province's early years, when comprehensive sex education, premarriage counselling, and obstetric care all fell under its rubric. Sterilization itself was closely linked to concurrent concerns of women's organizations, especially fears of immigration, agitation for birth control, and concern about the increase in the numbers of "feeble-minded."

Finally, the subject of eugenic sterilization was implicitly female, even though the procedure was carried out on both sexes. Abstract discussions of sterilization might be superficially ungendered; yet the case studies, examples, and tales told in the process of sterilization advocacy made it clear that sterilization was primarily to be done to and for women. Reproductive problems were to be addressed primarily through women's bodies rather than men's, at least within the social imaginary prevailing at the time of the act, if not in the actual consequences of the act itself. This powerful gendering of sterilization in Alberta was enabled by the ambivalent views Albertans held about hereditarianism, as well as by the popularity of "euthenics" (as well as eugenics) as a rationale for sterilization. Sterilization was attractive to mainstream Alberta not simply because it held the promise of winnowing out "bad" genetic strains; it also was about stopping women from becoming inappropriate mothers, or, if it was too late to prevent them, stopping them from continuing a disordered mothering career.

These elements of the social imaginary surrounding reproduction enabled the Sexual Sterilization Act to be defined as an important achievement by women, and less overtly as an important achievement *for* women, especially during the dry, impoverished, and vulnerable years of the 1920s, when drastic measures seemed necessary to stem the tide of immiseration. As a consequence, one of the largest human rights violations in Canadian history, and one of the world's most extensive programs of reproductive alteration, was able to root itself in the soil of interwar Alberta.

5 "Perhaps You May Think Me Independent": The Right to Mothers' Allowance

Introduction

In this chapter, we move from the troubles surrounding births to troubles that attached themselves to women because of their status as mothers. I have argued that reproduction was treated as the moral responsibility of women but also as the contested obligation of men and the precarious necessity of the state. In this chapter, I develop my understanding of these latter two terms – the obligations of men (often conspicuous by their abrogation), and the needs of the state – to examine how the political economy of reproduction extends beyond the moment of producing new people, into the work of supporting and caring for them.

I focus on debates about the provision of mothers' allowances to mothers who lacked ties to a male breadwinner, following the enactment of the Mothers' Allowance Act in Alberta in 1919. I draw on material from around Alberta, but concentrate on two main sources: the correspondence between individual citizens and the office of the provincial Attorney General, which shared the responsibility of administering the allowance; and the case files and correspondence of the Edmonton Board of Public Welfare (EBPW), which discussed and debated individual cases of women seeking the allowance. These two sources correspond to the two main bureaucracies involved in administering mothers' allowance programs: the municipal and provincial social welfare institutions.

After the mid-1920s, changes in the way public welfare in Alberta was financed meant that responsibility for mothers and children became more standardized and rationalized as it was shifted more and more to the provincial government, with less involvement by local municipalities, and eventually folded into broader social welfare bureaucracies, leaving fewer archival traces of correspondence and debate about mothers and children. Therefore, this chapter is confined mainly to the 1910s and 1920s.

Mothers' allowances represented a particular manifestation of "baby trouble," as children turned women into problematic citizens. Children made it impossible for women to be self-sufficient: they could not, nor were they expected to, sustain themselves on their own efforts or their own wages, because care of children was presumed to take precedence. When privatized dependence on a male breadwinner became impossible, the presence of young children forced women into relations of dependence on the state. The normative ideal of the times was for that relation of dependence to be privatized, in the form of marriages in which husbands were expected and indeed legally required to support the wives who produced and raised the children. But when this privatized normative relation broke down, the sustenance of mothers and children became a collective and public conundrum. How was the production of children to be subsidized and supported? Whose responsibility did mothers become when they broke (or were broken) out of the marital dyad? How would social reproduction, essential to the survival of Alberta, happen?

When men could not be forced to acknowledge their responsibilities to provide resources for social reproduction, the state, at provincial and municipal levels, had to step in to assume responsibilities, driven both by charitable imperatives to relieve the suffering of women and children and by the political-economic imperative to see that good citizens were produced. Mothers entered into a relation with municipal and provincial authorities that mimicked the gendered relations of dependence in the normative heterosexual relationship at the time. The state thus took on an essentially masculine position vis-à-vis mothers without men, standing in for the husband.

The mothers' allowance system in the early twentieth century was inescapably gendered. These were *mothers'* allowances, not parents' allowances, and were doled out to an entirely female group of recipients by an (almost) entirely male bureaucracy. A few women worked in the mothers' allowance machinery as "lady visitors" who inspected the homes of recipients or as secretaries to the boards that oversaw them, but beyond these few, there was almost perfect gender asymmetry in the mothers' allowance program, corresponding to the division of authority in traditional heterosexual marriages. Men as a group occupied the role of provider; women as a group were dependants.

This empirical observation is consistent with the feminist literature on state supports for child-raising, and indeed on social welfare in general. This literature tends to stress powerful ideologies of gender at work within ostensibly neutral and rational state programs; it also emphasizes the reification of particular ideals of masculinity and, especially, femininity within these programs. Wendy Brown's 1992 article "Finding the Man in the State" epitomizes this distinctively feminist approach to studying welfare. In her work, as in the work of others inspired by it, the state is intrinsically masculine and exists in a hierarchical relationship to a feminized and predominantly female group of citizens/dependants. The very titles of articles following Brown emphasize this gendered equation – an example is Kandaswamy's "You Trade In a Man for The Man: Domestic Violence and the US Welfare State" (2010), which posits that welfare and state support were continuations of domestic patriarchy by other means. Even those historians who do not see welfare programs as exclusively or primarily oppressive have tended to see the effects of these programs primarily in gendered terms, as having the potential to change, in unintended ways, the terms of women's dependence on individual men or on collective formations of masculine power (see, for example, Abramovitz 1996; Gordon 1994).

This attention to the gendering of state programs serves as a powerful corrective to the myth of a rational, functional, and disinterested state. But using gender relations as the principal lens through which to view such programs runs the risk of occluding other powerful dynamics at work. Marxist sociologists such as Ann Orloff have stressed other dimensions of the state provider/women recipients nature of welfare, emphasizing that gender is one of several dynamics at work (Orloff 1996). More recently, Canadian and American scholars have examined the economic dimensions of welfare policies that treat women not only as gendered individuals with marriage-like connections to the state, but also as potential workers whose labour is potentially mobilized by welfare policies (e.g. Jenson and Simeau 2003, Bezanson and Luxton 2006).

In this chapter, I hew closely to a primarily economic interpretation of state support for mothers' allowances, based on the idea that these allowances were embedded in a logic in which the labour of workers – mothers – was exploited to create "good citizens," that is, the children those mothers were raising. In this analysis, mothers' relationship to the state is as analogous to workers' relationship to employers as it is to women's relationship to men. Such a relationship, even within a capitalist logic, can never be ungendered, given that biology and social formation work together to ensure that women will always comprise the great majority of the "workers." However, by stressing that the story of mothers' allowances is a story about producing people as much as a story about gender, we add multidimensionality and complexity to accounts of these historical relationships.

Analysing the story of mothers' allowances as being about the production of useful new people is neither necessary nor inevitable. But as I will show, there is evidence that this perspective is consistent with the ways in which the main players in the dramas surrounding mothers' allowances in the early twentieth century viewed their activities. Mothers without male partners were being paid by the state to provide the necessary labour for the creation of a valuable product: healthy, morally upstanding children, precious resources for Alberta. The policing of women's gendered morality and conduct was important only insofar as it enhanced or hindered the creation of this product. Mothers' allowances were justified in that they remunerated women for performing the labour required to create good citizens. The system situated these mothers as workers rather than as moral agents in their own right.

The end-product of women's labour was good future citizens, and where individual men could not or would not provide women with the financial resources and incentives to carry out this work, the state would step in. In this sense, the local public welfare boards, along with the provincial government, served as the "husband of last resort" for women whose privatized relations of reproduction had failed them. These boards, however, can also be seen as employers of last resort, paying mothers to produce good citizens when such citizens could not be successfully produced within privatized relations of reproduction.

Telling this story of the relations between women as a group and "the state" as an entity summons these questions: Who were the women? And what was this thing called "the state" in interwar Alberta? The women in question were of course not *all* the women of Alberta; rather, they were those whose heteronormative trajectory had gone off-track – either they had reproduced without securing the support of an individual man, or, having secured that support, they had lost it through misdeed or misfortune. These single mothers thus existed both inside and outside the ideal form of the Alberta family – they might be deviant as women and wives, but as mothers, they were the guardians of the province's most precious resource.

Who, then, was the state? Theories of the state abound, and it is not my intention to review them here. A more useful approach is to start from the assumption that states, whether federal,[1] provincial, or municipal, are complex, internally contradictory, and constitutive of social relations, and then to consider how the state bureaucracy might have appeared to differently situated Albertans at the end of the First World War.

Immigrants from Germany or elsewhere in Eastern Europe might experience the government of Alberta primarily as an enforcer of marginalization, as they were interned in the poultry buildings at the Lethbridge municipal exhibition grounds. Coal miners in southern Alberta might have similar experiences, as the province mobilized strikebreakers and police to combat labour unrest in 1919. African American settlers coming up from Oklahoma to escape Jim Crow laws and settle at Amber Valley in northern Alberta saw a similar face; they were harassed and discouraged at the border and in their journeys north by official agents.

For grain farmers in central Alberta, whose harvests increased dramatically towards the end of the war when the demand for grain was artificially inflated, the provincial government facilitated their capture of markets through extension services and encouragements to take up land and settle; it also helped them ship their crops to potential buyers. But in the years following the war, farmers' interactions with the state grew tense and conflicted. The demand for a wheat pool to stabilize prices swept through the grassroots and eventually resulted in the establishment of the Alberta Wheat Pool in 1923. By contrast, for men and women in imbued with zeal for social reform, especially with a religious inflection, the state was the site of struggle over the prohibition of social evils and vices, especially when it came to temperance legislation. Such a law, which outlawed alcohol (except under strictly controlled circumstances), was finally passed in 1916.

The Alberta government was thus simultaneously radical and repressive, emancipatory and racist, depending on who was engaging with the province's various bureaucracies and what the stakes were. This complexity is evident in the experiences of the women whose stories form the basis of this chapter. For most of these women, "the state" as an entity was essentially meaningless. They experienced state power as personalized, mediated through the members of the welfare boards that decided on their fates, the friends and neighbours who petitioned on their behalf (or who turned them in for non-compliance), and the semi-professionalized "lady visitors" and proto-social workers who surveilled them.

The province's small population and relative lack of formal bureaucracy meant that the terms of engagement between dependent mothers and those who had the means to assist them often had to be negotiated individually and repeatedly. Officials could be stingy or generous. Decisions in the name of the people of Alberta were often made by the civic-minded volunteers who sat on public welfare boards rather than by career civil servants. Also, different levels of government came into conflict, with the financial responsibility for these women shifting back and forth between municipal and provincial boards. The relationship between the recipients of mothers' allowances and those who doled them out was oddly intimate, shaped by narratives of virtue or disaster, closely tied to individual idiosyncrasies, and endlessly renegotiated, with women seeking to maximize their entitlements and welfare boards seeking to minimize them.

I begin this chapter by outlining the Mothers' Allowance Act and then backtrack to describe the context from which it emerged. The mothers' allowance program in Alberta was shaped by economic, institutional, social, and even environmental trends that manifested themselves in three distinct but related socio-economic contexts: the "perfect storm" of disasters affecting the viability of nuclear households in the second and third decades of the twentieth century; the crisis tendencies in Alberta's gender regime in the same decades; and state responsibility for soldiers' dependants following the First World War.

I then provide a snapshot of the women who sought mothers' allowances and of the tussling between groups of powerful men regarding who was to pay for these women's reproductive activities. I also present the perspectives of the municipal authorities who doled out the allowances, treating them as a form of fee-for-service that paid for the work of social reproduction. Finally, I turn to the challenge faced by all women who sought allowances – the imperative to be both a "good worker," efficient and productive in the creation of high-quality children, and a "good woman," sexually abstemious when no man was in the picture, yet receptive and available to a husband. Throughout the chapter, I focus on the stories revealed through the records of the EBPW, the largest and most active entity tasked with assisting these mothers, with some forays into other parts of the province.

The Alberta Mothers' Allowance Act

Alberta's first Mothers' Allowance Act came into existence in 1919. The initial act stated simply that a woman with children whose husband was dead or insane could apply to her municipality for relief. Upon inspection and assessment of her case, she could receive an allowance of an unspecified amount as long as she agreed to repeat visits (in practice, usually once every three months) and complied with conditions laid down by the municipal public welfare board. The act was amended in 1926 to allow women whose husbands were completely incapacitated and likely to remain so for at least a year to apply as well. The amount spent on allowances rose rapidly. In 1919, 245 women received allowances totalling $39,470.04, but within six years the number had more than tripled, with 825 women receiving allowances totalling $283,595.50 ("Mothers Allowance Payment Acts Larger than Ever in 1925," *Wetaskiwin Times*, 1 April 1926, 8).

Alberta offers especially rich documentation of mothers' allowances because the provincial system was quite unstandardized. Other jurisdictions in Canada had consistent regulations on matters such as the amount of property a woman could own and still be considered eligible for an allowance, or how much money per month she could receive, or what the maximum or minimum allowances could be. Alberta had no such rules: most decisions were left up to local municipal boards of public welfare – a circumstance that generated substantial discussions of individual cases. For example, the Battle River Municipal District met on 8 December 1932 and determined that one woman's allowance be reduced to $15 per month, and another's to $17.50; two others were to be given $30 per month, and one other's was to be administered directly by the municipality and not given to her in cash "as this council feels that some supervision is necessary in her case" ("Council Members of Battle River MD Adjudicate on Mothers' Allowance," *Irma Times*, 23 December 1932, 1).

Alberta law also specified that half the cost of allowances would be met by the applicant's municipality. This generated substantial discussion of individual cases and whether cases could be offloaded to other municipalities, or removed from municipal rolls altogether. Municipalities were also responsible for appointing and paying inspectors to ensure that only deserving mothers received the allowances. This division of responsibility generated voluminous correspondence among municipalities, the attorney general's office, and the provincial

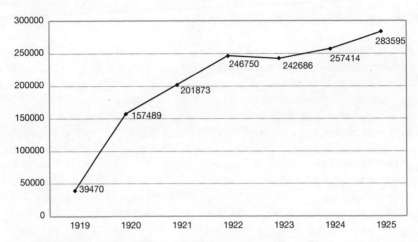

5.1 Provincial expenditures ($) on Mothers' Allowances, 1919–25 ("Mothers' Allowance Payments").

Source: *The UFA*, 4 March 1926, 16

Superintendent of Mothers' Allowances, who was often also the Superintendent of Neglected and Delinquent Children. Much of that correspondence consisted of complaints from municipalities that cases were being foisted on them by the provincial bureaucracy or that reimbursements for their share of the allowances were being delayed.[2] The parameters of the Mothers' Allowance were also contested between the province and the municipalities, with the province tending to favour a more liberal interpretation of who could be considered a deserving candidate, and the municipalities tending towards a narrower vision.[3]

The 1910s: The "Perfect Storm"

The 1910s were a disastrous time for nuclear families in Alberta, especially those newly arrived from other countries, who lacked informal safety nets. The Canadian government's overselling of Alberta as an agrarian paradise had drawn many impoverished families to the province from Britain and Europe, who arrived only to find themselves thrown back on their own inadequate resources. The EBPW minutes often refer to settlement schemes, mainly originating in the British Isles, such as the Hebridean Settlement Scheme, which had failed and left its members broke and stranded. The crash of the land boom in 1913 left many men with high mortgage payments just as the realization was sinking in that they would be unable to make a go of farming marshy, arid, or unirrigatable land. Jones (2005, 381) recounts a joke that circulated in late 1912: "'Mary,' said the sick man to his wife, after being diagnosed with smallpox, 'if any of my creditors call tell them I am at last in a position to give them something.'"

For men who had purchased land at the inflated prices of the prewar land boom, a bad season could mean they were unable to make the mortgage payments. Many of them then left the farm in search of paid employment, often in the United States, and did not return. Even in years of good harvests, disaster could strike rural households when men deserted in the fall, taking with them the proceeds from selling that year's harvest and leaving their families to the vicissitudes of the winter (Cavanaugh 1993, 208). The winter of 1914–15 was notoriously severe and drove many rural families into towns for shelter. The following spring, floods destroyed settlements on riverbanks. These settlements were often the site of low-income neighbourhoods (e.g., Edmonton's River Flats), and their destruction exacerbated the residents' poverty.

The outbreak of the First World War produced some short-term benefits, such as an increase in prices for farmers, but after good rains in 1916, drought conditions set in. The war also created a sharp short-term drop in urban employment, as many construction and civic infrastructure projects employing unskilled and semi-skilled men were terminated in order to divert money and resources to the national war effort. The war did provide a medium-term source of income for some families, as men joined up in recruiting drives, but the extremely high casualty rates and the failure of some soldiers to return to their families rapidly undid any benefits from a wartime economy.

More than 49,000 Albertans – nearly 10 per cent of the provincial population – eventually served in the war. More significantly, from the perspective of household stability, 35 per cent of all men between eighteen and forty-five enlisted, with Edmonton leading the nation by providing 13,000 volunteers (Bright 2005, 215). Not all of these men returned, and of those who did, not all of them returned in the same condition as they had left. The physical and psychological damage of the war was linked to increasing numbers of men deserting their families.

While men were in active service, their families received payments from the federal Canadian Patriotic Fund. When the men were demobilized and returned, that assistance was cut back sharply, even though the men might not be able to return to their former occupations. This led to riots by veterans in Calgary. This issue of "deserting soldiers" appears repeatedly in the minutes of bodies tasked with finding solutions for impoverished mothers and families. The EBPW, in its 1917 annual report, stressed the increasing number of cases of "soldier desertion in which the solider husbands have defaulted and created situations of unnecessary difficulty and suffering ... There is reason to expect that the board will have occasion to serve in an increasingly number of soldier cases as time goes on" (City of Edmonton Archives, RG 24, box 1, file 1).

After the war, the high prices that had buffered some farmers against economic uncertainty stayed high, leading to broad discontent and difficulty for families in meeting their daily needs. Labour unrest spread throughout the province, especially in the south, driven by material fears, including "the massive wartime increase in prices of goods which had risen as high as 70 percent, shortages of basic goods, and fears of unemployment as soldiers returned to reclaim their jobs" (Bright 2005, 425). As rapidly as they had risen, producer prices for wheat crashed in the early 1920s, from $2.31 a bushel in 1919 to 77 cents in 1922 (Rennie 2005, 452). This provided some temporary relief for those who lived in towns and were net purchasers of grain products, but for those who farmed, this was another calamity.

As the war wound to a close, the Spanish flu pandemic reached Alberta. Those who were able to recover from the influenza were often incapacitated for protracted periods, leading to failures to get in a crop or to make mortgage payments. All of these crises converged to produce a spike in the number of women and children who were unsupported by men, and who eventually became the clients of welfare programs.

The Edmonton Central Relief Committee, the first organized, broad-based secular effort to provide support to needy families, grew out of this "perfect storm." It began as pooled contributions of Edmonton businessmen to relieve the sufferings of the winter of 1914, and solidified into a permanent municipal body, the EBPW, later that year. The board had an extremely corporatist membership, dominated by prominent businessmen and retailers, and invited "anyone knowing of cases of destitution" to advise their office ("Edmonton Public Welfare Board is in Working Order," *Edmonton Bulletin*, 16 September 1914, 1). Its documents repeatedly refer to its members as "leading businessmen" or "prominent citizens." Its composition was entirely male, although it employed the services of "lady visitors" to supervise women receiving the mothers' allowance, and its long-term secretary was one Florence King, who managed much of the daily work of transferring allowances.

The 1910s: Crisis Tendencies in Gender Relations

In addition to this series of economic and environmental catastrophes, the 1910s were a time when gender strife came to the forefront. Useful here is the concept of "crisis tendencies," referring to internal tensions that force to the surface the discontent and incongruities inherent in particular arrangements, but without compelling a wholesale trans- formation (cf. Connell's [1998] appropriation of Habermas). The best- known example of this with regard to gender is woman suffrage, which has become a touchstone of mainstream Canadian history and which is used to mark a moment in the march towards equity and emancipation for women.

While woman suffrage has captured much popular and scholarly attention, the controversies around the lesser-known 1917 Dower Act are much more relevant to the context in which the Mothers' Allow- ance Act emerged several years later. The importance of the Dower Act to the philosophy and ideology of the Mothers' Allowance Act cannot be overstated. The 1917 Dower Act specified that wives could not be dispossessed of their family residence by their husband with- out their consent and gave widows a life interest in their deceased husband's property. This act came into existence in the wake of the same crises that led to the Mothers' Allowance Act – crises that had been exacerbated by the land boom of the prewar period during which men sold out their farms to the highest bidder and then aban- doned their wives and children to be turned off the land by the new owners (Cavanaugh 1993, 212). In the words of historian Catherine Cavanaugh, the fight for the Dower Act was "a direct assault on arbi- trary male privilege that guaranteed sole possession of the family as- sets to the husband" (ibid., 215). More than the better-known suffrage campaign, the struggle for dower rights decentred men from the sur- vival of women and children – a move that prefigured the Mothers' Allowance Act, through which the state stepped in to sustain mothers and their children.

Many of the individuals and organizations that supported the 1919 Mothers' Allowance Act, such as Emily Murphy and the United Farm Women of Alberta, had earlier pushed for the Dower Act. In both cases, financial support for women was justified on the grounds that women's work of social reproduction was not being adequately remunerated by the market and thus needed recognition and protection by the state. However, the Mothers' Allowance Act pushed the Dower Act one step further. While the Dower Act focused on women's past contributions to social reproduction – working with their husbands to create a viable household and "proving up" the homestead claim – the Mothers' Allowance Act focused on women's present and future contributions by paying them for their ongoing work. Women did not have to earn their way into eligibility for mothers' allowance through their past efforts – they qualified based on their status at the moment they applied for the allowance.

A second difference between the Dower Act and the suffrage struggle – one with more material significance – is that while the Dower Act provided the legal basis for women to claim rights in their marital home, it did not actually provide for the transfer of resources from the state to individual women. The Mothers' Allowance Act took this logic one step further and established the province not just as the guarantor of women's legal rights but also as the supplier of sustenance for mothers and children.

Women's groups strongly supported the Dower Act. However, when we read through letters to the provincial government complaining about the act, it appears that many men believed this legislation set up conditions in which women could demand more and more concessions from men, with the provincial government, through the Dower Act, acting as guarantor. Letters of complaint sent to the attorney general by men opposed to the act paint a picture of women who were determined to get whatever material property they could and who no longer needed a man to legitimate their claims. One man wrote as follows to the attorney general:

> I would like some advice as to how to go about the matter and troubles I have. My wife has got to be master sins [sic] the [Dower] law came in place that she has half the homestead. She takes away [illegible] and don't do [illegible]. She goes when she pleases and comes back the same. She has been away 19 weeks today. I might have been out working if she had stayed at home. I have to stay home to look after three head of horses and other things she could have looked after easy without any trouble to her. She is staying with a young man who is living with his father and mother under the idea that she is looking after his mother; you may go any time of day and catch her coming out of his bedroom ... She knows I am helpless and with three bad crops in the last year I am stuck fast. I am not alone, there is another man who had the same troubles as me. (letter, 24 February 1917, PAA 75.126 1106)

Another man wrote:

> It is to be hoped that you will make the dower law so satisfactory at this
> session of the legislature that these women will stop harping on equal
> property rights. Some of these women ... are going to place in peril every
> home in Alberta. ... It is now a case where I can hardly have a bite of an
> apple unless I give her a bite of mine. A woman frankly confessed this to
> me. She said they were determined to be better protected for property
> rights ... If these women have the law changed, why dozens of homes in
> Alberta would be broken up and people would lose all. (letter, 14 February
> 1920, PAA 75.126 1108)

These dynamics were amplified in the debates around the Mothers'
Allowance Act, which came two years after the Dower Act. One the one
side, we see general sympathy for and awareness of the plight of deserted women. On the other, we see a backlash against women who
used their status as mothers to leverage their claims to legal and financial support.

The 1910s: Soldiers and Mothers

The Mothers' Allowance Act benefited from the Dower Act, which pio-
neered the principle of independent financial existence for mothers
with children. But it also benefited from the extension of welfare entitlements, which swelled in the wake of pensions for soldiers and their
widows. This was a slow process of widening the circle of entitlement:
from women whose husbands died fighting for the country, to women
whose husbands died in other ways, to women whose husbands might
not be physically dead but were effectively dead in social and financial
terms, because they were not physically present and could not be found
and provided no support to their families.

Organizations representing the women (and some men) who had
benefited from the patriotic compensation paid to the relatives of those
who died in the First World War called for the extension of financial support to other destitute women. The Great War Next of Kin Association
of Calgary, for instance, passed repeated resolutions drawing analogies
between the situation of next of kin who received pensions and the situations of families that had not been so fortunate as to have a war to
blame for the loss of their husband. This analogy between mothers and
soldiers should come as no surprise to readers.

The Calgary Next of Kin Association sent a letter to the province's Legislative Assembly, leveraging their moral authority and "urg[ing] upon the provincial legislature the need to escalate the scope of the proposed Mothers' Allowance Act to include all needy mothers" (letter, 21 February 1919, PAA 75.126 1106). The Medicine Hat branch of this organization took a similar stance:

> Whereas several cases have come before this branch of the GWVA recently in which women have been deserted by their husbands, and whereas there is apparently no fund from which these women can obtain support unless in the case of a returned soldier the soldier deserts his wife within three months or his rejoining her from the service, and whereas it would appear to us that a woman whose character is beyond reproach and who has a family to support ought to be entitled to relief under the provisions of the Mothers Pensions Act [sic], [we] ... petition the provincial government to request that the act be amended so as to include women of good character who have been deserted by their husbands through no fault of their own and who have a family to maintain and who are without any visible means of support. (letter, 16 March 1920, PAA 75.126 1106)

The Provincial Executive of the Councils of Women, an umbrella body representing a range of women's organizations, used the same logic to urge the extension of military pensions to allowances for mothers:

> As the child is the greatest asset of the state ... and therefore a mother who has been deprived by either the death, incapacity or other causes of the support of the father should not be compelled by necessity to neglect her children to her detriment in order to secure for them the necessities of life, it is therefore the duty of the state to relieve such conditions ... The proposed Mothers Allowance Act [should] be amended so as to include assistance to all needy mothers, *the amount of assistance to equal that paid to the widow and children of a soldier* (PAA 75.126 1106, 24 February 1919; emphasis added)

The EBPW went one step further than the Great War Next of Kin Association had done when it called for mothers' allowances to be indexed to military dependants' pensions. The board equated the work of mothers directly to the services rendered by soldiers, recommending that mothers' allowances "be graded in accordance with the scale of the Dominion government army pensions to privates, namely $40 per month per woman" (minutes of 9 October 1919, MS 213.C.1, file 4).

This equation between mothers and soldiers, both of whom were understood as paid workers for the state, was reflected and amplified by the ways in which recipients of the mothers' allowance were discussed in provincial deliberations. When the topic of mothers' allowances came up in provincial debate, agents of the government were quite explicit about how they viewed the women seeking mothers' allowances, situating them as undertaking services for the state, in that they raised children, for which they would be financially compensated. This rhetoric defined the state as the owner, or at best the steward, of the products of this work of social reproduction, in the form of children who would become good citizens.

In 1917 the provincial Superintendent of Neglected Children, a strong advocate of mothers' allowances, wrote: "It is generally recognized that it is the state's duty to see that mothers who make a valuable contribution to the human wealth of the community in rearing boys and girls to reputable manhood and womanhood should be provided for in a suitable way" (Annual Report of the Superintendent of Neglected Children 1917, 8).

The following year, just before the Mothers' Allowance Act was passed, he pressed the point further in his annual report, insisting that "the theory of mothers' allowances is that children are the state's most valuable asset and as its most priceless resource must be conserved" (Annual Report of the Superintendent of Neglected Children 1918).

After the act was passed, the same rhetoric of productivity and of children as state assets ran through government pronouncements on the strategic significance of allowances. This rhetoric would remain consistent even as the party in power shifted from the Liberals to the more populist United Farmers of Alberta. In the official organ of the UFA, one editorialist wrote: "The government has consistently kept in mind that the boys and girls growing up in Alberta are, from the standpoint of the Province, an asset taking priority over the resources of forest, field and mine. To that end, the grants to mothers with dependent children have increased from year to year" ("Boys and Girls Greatest Asset," *The UFA*, 10 June 1926, 4).

Mothers on Relief

Women came into the mothers' allowance program in several different ways. Some brought their own situation to the attention of municipal authorities or the provincial government. For example, one woman wrote to Nellie McClung, the well-known advocate for women's concerns and Liberal member of the Legislative Assembly:

> Pardon me if I am presuming in writing to you of a matter which is only of interest to myself and my 2 babies. My husband left me two years ago and I only heard of him once since, and no support for 4 years scarcely. I have two little children both girls 3 and 5 years old. I heard my husband was dead but I have not been able to find any assurance of this as it seems he went under another name … It is almost impossible to keep up at times, the strain is so great, and it is impossible to keep my babies properly. I do not want to have this matter made public, but I'm willing to give you all the information you will want on this subject. Please reply as soon as possible. But please give me no hope if there is none to give. (letter, 20 March 1923, PAA 75.126 7646, Mothers' Allowance general file)

McClung referred her to her municipal council for help.

In their appeals, most women stressed how hard they worked, how their various attempts to keep themselves and their children fed and sheltered had been thwarted by circumstance, and the length of time they had been struggling on their own before turning to outsiders for help. They presented themselves as competent, capable individuals caught up in calamities outside their control. The "ideal" candidate for mothers' allowance was a wife or mother who had been deserted or whose husband was incapacitated to the point that he could not carry out his husbandly function. These "ideal" candidates had been thrown into destitution not through fault of their own but by force of circumstance. They were making every effort to climb out of their abyss but were in need of assistance. Women who successfully presented themselves in this way were more likely to be deemed worthy of assistance than those who appeared to be simply poor or feckless.

One such woman wrote directly to the provincial attorney general, describing the "perfect storm" of complex economic, environmental, and medical calamities that had befallen her:

> My husband died two years before of the flu – he left a half section of land partly paid for. After his death I tried to run things by myself, I sure worked hard to try and make a living for my two children but that year I was dried out and lost everything I had, having hired help and boarding them and getting no return from the land. The next year I rented my place and didn't make enough to pay interest to say nothing of taxes and

insurance. I was compelled to sell the land, and now I have to make a living and it's very hard to get a position with two children and my girl had to go to school. Luck seems dead against me. I was very anxious to keep the farm for my kiddies but my animals laid down and died, and the price of pigs came down, chickens got disease amongst them, the price of oats came down and oats was all I had. The hired help took every advantage they could of me. My husband before his death signed up two [promissory] notes with some neighbours which I have had to pay. My little girl met with an accident and both of them have whooping cough and to crown all I am compelled to ask for charity – but it's for my children and I would do anything to keep them with me, for if you don't help me I shall have to place them in an orphanage. Like seems like one darn thing after another. I have tried to be brief, and I can prove all I say. (letter, 12 December 1922, PAA73.126 File 762)

Another woman wrote to the attorney general to contest a recommendation by the municipal inspector that her pension be reduced, describing a series of calamities that had begun with a dropped cigarette that ignited a grassfire that destroyed her crops. This letter is worth quoting in detail not only because it details women's sense of entitlement to support for their work as mothers, but also because the writer ends by invoking a prominent local man with deep investments in the community to vouch for the worthiness of her claim. Such men – presumably representatives of Alberta's public interest – were often called on to confirm women's descriptions of their situations and to verify that the women were indeed hard workers and good producers:

I write to you about my pension. [The municipal welfare inspector] thought I should have my pension cut down, he said there were so many more that needed it but under the circumstances I do not see how I possibly can. Last fall I had a good wheat crop but only had a few loads hauled away when we took down with scarletina … and it has taken all we can rake up just to keep the stock alive. … Now we are in the same disease again for three weeks. God only knows how long, yet two have it. The oldest boy and the girl are aged 10 years and just before this the oldest girl had a very serious operation which cost me a lot and no doctor's bill paid yet. This is the third hospital bill I have had in two years. We have no one to help us, only the boy who is 16 now in January … I only ask for the pension to run as it is for a while yet say until next harvest and see how everything is. If you care to write to Mr F, the banker in D., he will tell you how things are, in fact he said he would write you. (letter, 2 January 1922, PAA 75.126 7646, Mothers' Allowance general file).

Prominent local men such as the banker in D. advocated for mothers in distress, mediating their entitlement to support from the provincial and municipal governments. One such letter came to the provincial attorney general from Salmon and West General Merchants in the town of Etzikom:

> There is a family living about a mile from this town who are in bad shape. There are seven children, the oldest is 14 and the youngest is 11 months old. The father had the misfortune of having both feet frozen in 1917 and both feet had to be amputated. Also one hand was so badly frozen that all the fingers were removed, this is the right hand. These people are in a destitute condition and the mother was in the store today and said she was baking the last batch of flour in the house. (letter, 13 January 1922, PAA 75.126 7646, Mothers' Allowance General File)

The letters from these men often focused on the deficiencies of the husband who had abandoned the family, even as letters written by the women themselves were usually silent on the deficiencies of their former partners. Presumably, it took an upright, respectable man to judge another man's character. One such letter came from the manager of the Merchant's Bank in Delburne:

> There is a deserving case in this district of a widow with eight young children which will number nine in a few months whose husband died last week. She has been left without means except for a few horses, some cattle and machinery ... All they will have to live on is the revenue from five or six milch [cows] and the neighbours will assist in getting in a crop for her this year. The CPR [from which the deceased man had obtained a mortgage on the land] were taking proceedings at the time Mr B died to repossess the land, Mr B being worthless and shiftless. However I have persuaded the CPR to withdraw proceedings and grant the widow an extension on her contract for seven more years which should help her considerably as the farm is a good one and with help for a few years she should be able to make it pay and keep the family together if she is entitled to a pension and I believe she ought to be after having been in this district 13 ½ years and a hard worker herself. (letter, 23 March 1920, PAA 73.126, file 761)

In other towns, the local branch of the UFA brought forward the cases of deserving women, usually emphasizing the sympathy of the people of the district for the woman in question, and echoing the UFA's ideological investments in reciprocity and mutual help. One such example came from Lost Lake, where the postmaster wrote that

> we have a young widow and three small children left on our hands without any money ... The members of Lost Lake UFA gave him a decent burial and are looking after her and the children but we are all poor ourselves and cannot afford to keep her very long. The settlers are going to make a bee this spring and break enough [ground] and seed it but this won't feed her and her children ... This is a deserving case. Hoping to hear from you. (2 February 1924, PAA 73.126, file 763)

Such letters suggest powerful local solidarity around the figure of the destitute mother. However, other letters suggest intra-community resentments and conflicts over the payment of mothers' allowances, despite the official rhetoric about producing good citizens through payments to their mothers. One life insurance agent wrote angrily to the attorney general that the mothers' allowances were cutting into his business because

> we have on several occasions met with the statement that life insurance was a poor proposition owing to the fact that the man who was thrifty and left his family supplied with life insurance was penalized for doing so, inasmuch as his family not only received no support from the government on account of their possession of life insurance but had to pay through taxes for the support of widows and orphans of those who had not been so thrifty. (letter from DA Smith Insurance Agency, 11 June 1923, PAA 75.126 7646, Mothers' Allowance General File)

Other indignant citizens complained that women receiving mothers' allowance pensions owned their own homes and had enough money to pay mortgages, or that they had not liquidated enough of their property to be considered truly destitute. Because these allowances were handled on a case-by-case basis with little standardization, with the expenditures often published in local papers, it was not difficult for neighbourhood busybodies to find out who was getting how much money. In particular, local opinion could be roused when a woman receiving mothers' allowance was perceived to be better off financially than her neighbours. In the case of Mrs O, who lived in the Peace River district, neighbours complained to a local councilor, who then wrote to the provincial government that "as three of [her sons] are living at home and strong husky lads, she is really better off than most of her neighbours in as far as she has ample labour to work her farm and judging from the amount of entertaining done, is not suffering from lack of means" (letter from Municipal Treasurer of the Peace District, 29 April 1929, PR 1971.336/120).

Mrs O continued to press her claim for Mothers' Allowance, and to raise the ire of her neighbours, who reported that she had the labour of her sons to depend on. Furthermore, her frequent "entertaining" was not of the wholesome sort and was in fact being encouraged by her adult daughters, who were "living a life of easy virtue in Edmonton" (letter from Municipal Treasurer of the Peace District, 29 July 1929, PR 1971.336/120). Mrs O never did receive the allowance she sought.

In one case, the Social Service Council of Alberta attempted to intervene with the Superintendent of Mothers' Allowances on behalf of a woman, Mrs P, who was the subject of a petition circulating in her district calling for her to be removed from the allowance rolls. The council claimed that "a petition is being circulated her in an endeavour to stop her pension ... People here have the idea that it will raise their taxes ... [and] it must be admitted that Mrs P is in somewhat better circumstances than many men who are not in receipt of government aid" (letter, 26 January 1922, PAA 75.126 7646, Mothers' Allowance general file).

Such complaints were almost always about the inequity and inefficiency of keeping women on the rolls who already had assets, rather than about the quality of their mothering. Municipal councils complained to the province about women who had made an end run around the municipal bureaucracy by appealing directly to the Attorney General or the Superintendent of Neglected Children for assistance; or who had moved from one district to another to take advantage of a supposedly more lenient and generous municipal administration; or who had begun earning money on their own while still receiving the allowance.

With respect to the latter, one local inspector wrote to the Superintendent of Neglected Children about a town that did not want to pay its share for a woman who had been seen earning money:

Council said they understood the allowance was granted in order to keep the mother at home with her children. They complained that Mrs C was not doing this and that she had been out cooking for a threshing outfit that fall. I explained to them that their contention was correct but in the case of Mrs C who only received $45 per month and had four children eligible for an allowance it was impossible at the present time to keep he family together without doing a little work to supplement her allowance. If it was council's wish that she remain at home all the time, I would have to increase her allowance. They agreed the amount was too small for her to manage entirely without working and withdrew their objection in this respect. (report from local inspector, 30 November 1920, PAA 73.126, file 762)

As the 1920s wore on and the environmental and economic disasters in the southern part of the province gathered steam, some local governments protested that they were entirely unable to pay their share of the allowance. Cities as large as Fort McLeod, a major commercial centre in the southeast of the province, went bankrupt, as did smaller units. The secretary-treasurer of the village of Richdale attached a poignant note to his explanation of their precarious financial position, pointing out that "the financial position is practically untenable at the time. Might add that if it were not for the widows [sic] allowance being wished on us that we would be able to scratch along until the possible improvement of the times, your department must know what we have been up against, weathering the storm for six dry years" (letter, 28 November 1923, PAA 73.126, file 763).

Municipal Authorities and Social Reproduction

Once the Mothers' Allowance Act was enacted, the municipal and provincial authorities concerned were quite clear about what they expected to get for their money: they were paying women to produce children for the province. Their interests lay in the efficient production of a labour force. The EBPW, for example, framed its mothers' allowance work – both its advocacy for the passage of the act and its administrative tasks after it had been passed – squarely within the rhetoric of production and efficiency. In its 1919 report, just after the act had passed, it congratulated itself:

After four year of steady propaganda work the board has had the satisfaction of seeing the Mothers' Allowance Act ... The board holds this to be the most important of its present activities as well as that from which the most satisfactory result[s] may reasonably be hoped. The act is aimed entirely at child welfare and it is the ideal before the board to obtain such co-operation from the mother ... as to equip the fatherless child mentally morally and physical [so] that *his future value to the country will outweigh immeasurably the present expenditure on his behalf.* (Annual Report of Board of Public Welfare 1919, 3, Edmonton City Archives, RG 24, box 1, file 1; emphasis added)

Within this framework, inefficiency or inadequate inputs to the work of childrearing could not be tolerated. A woman could have her request for an allowance turned down on the grounds that she was "unlikely to prove efficient as a Mothers' Allowance case" (Edmonton City Archives, MC 213.C1, file 9). Case notes are filled with references to the recipient's effectiveness in doing the work for which she had been engaged: raising future citizens.

In its 1920 report, the board made it clear that the capacity for efficient and profitable social reproduction was the main criterion for receiving an allowance, trumping need, poverty, or bad luck:

The board considers that if the women by reason of her training, temperament or defect of any kind – mental, physical or moral – appears incapable of maintaining a home in which the children will have a reasonable chance of becoming worthy Canadian citizens, then neither poverty, sickness, misfortune nor any other consideration can in its opinion justify recommendations for allowances ... [for] the woman who is rearing several of the nation's future citizens ... The object before the board is to co-operate with the mother and to encourage her to make the most of every advantage that the city and the state can offer in the endeavour to equip the child in such manner *that his value to the community in future shall exceed the present expenditure on his behalf.* (Annual Report of Board of Public Welfare, City of Edmonton Archives, 1920, 7–8, RG 24, box 1, file 1; emphasis added)

The EBPW often reprimanded women or punished them by reducing their allowances if evidence was found that the women were not devoting enough time to caring for children at home, by working outside the home or even by undertaking work within the home that interfered with their primary job, which was to raise children. While women receiving the allowance were permitted, and even expected, to make some financial contributions, usually by taking in "homework" such as sewing or laundry, too much entrepreneurship was viewed as suspect, for it competed with their primary employment, which was raising children for the state. Lillie Young McKinney, a member of the Calgary YMCA commissioned by the attorney general's office to write a series of brochures for the public explaining the new domestic legislation that was being introduced, made it clear that raising children for the state was paid work and should not have to compete with other paid work: a woman receiving the Mothers' Allowance "should not have to work outside the home. *If she does, there is something abnormal in it.* She usually carries besides her outside work the burden of her household" (brochure, 10 February 1921, PAA 75.126, file 1107a; emphasis added).

In practice, women were often required to cut back their paid work, as meagre as it might be, as a condition of receiving the allowance.[4] For example, in the case of Mrs McD,

> [she] is a widow with four children under 13 years of age and there is evident danger of her being compelled to neglect her children through going out to work, on the understanding that Mrs McD will undertake only such work as will not interfere with her care of the children and the home, and that she attend to this duty in a way which will be satisfactory to the board, she [will] be granted assistance of $30 per month. (minutes, 10 April 1916, Edmonton City Archives, MS 213.C.1, file 4)

Unfortunately, Mrs McD proved not to be a good worker for social reproduction. The board received reports from neighbours that her children were rude and badly behaved. In September 1916, the board decided to cut off her allowance, not on the grounds that she no longer needed it or was now able to support her family financially, but "in view of the untrustworthiness of Mrs McD and her apparent inability to control her family" (minutes, 25 September 1916, Edmonton City Archives, MS 213.C.1, file 4). Mrs McD placed her two youngest children in an orphanage and came back to the Welfare Board to plead her case, saying that she would be able to control her children better now and requesting that her allowance be restarted. However, the board did not believe she would be able to do so, and the case was closed.

Mrs McD's experience was not unusual. The board often relied on accounts of children's misbehaviour – boys seen idling around pool halls, or girls who dressed inappropriately – as evidence that their mothers were not doing their jobs properly. If the mother could not raise a child properly, the usual recourse was to place the children in a series of local orphanages, which catered not only to orphans but also to children whose mothers had been cut off from the allowance. In many cases, the children cycled into and out of these orphanages as their mothers were able to convince the board that their child-raising skills had improved.

Mrs A had a similar experience. There was no dispute about the dire nature of her situation – she was a widow with nine children under the age of fourteen and no assets. Yet the board recommended against making her an allowance on the grounds that she was an "incompetent and dirty housewife, untruthful and not generally reliable" (minutes, May 1925, Edmonton City Archives, MS 213.C.1, file 13). The board recommended that "no person be paid at the present time, but that efforts be made to raise the standard of the home," after which an allowance might be considered. In other words, Mrs A's entitlement to state support was based not on her evident need but on her capacity to perform the labour of social reproduction.

In proffering, withdrawing, and adjusting the allowance granted to each woman, the EBPW was applying a carrot-and-stick approach to shape its recipients in two directions, towards two related yet not entirely compatible ideals. One was the ideal of the rational economic actor, the worker who provided for herself and her family as much as she could reasonably be expected to do, and who participated in the cash economy to the best of her ability as long as it did not compromise her primary job, which was raising her children. As noted above, the EBPW did not endorse the notion that mothers should be completely privatized within their homes, and it sanctioned women who were perceived to be attempting to withdraw entirely from the marketplace. The second ideal was that of the "good woman" in a patriarchal society, who sought and accepted male protection and authority in the form of legal marriage, and who abstained from relations with men outside legalized marriage.

Good Workers

Women receiving the allowance were expected to be good workers and to engage in paid labour as fully as possible, as long as this did not interfere with their primary job of caring for children. Women who made choices that the EPWB viewed as unreasonable – who refused work that was offered to them, or who were thought to not be putting enough effort into the work they did have – were described as "indifferent" or "wasteful" and were vulnerable to having their allowance cut off, even though there was no question that they and their children were in need. Threats to remove children from the home and to terminate financial support were used to guide women back onto the path of appropriate paid work. Mrs A, for instance, was a

> woman with two children of school age. This woman, who is a good tailor-ess but an indifferent housekeeper, has been assisted considerably in the past two years. Committee considers that it is in the best interests of this woman, who is not energetic ... that the children be placed in the Children's Aid home this winter and the mother seek a position which will maintain herself and at least help maintain the children. Further assistance is to be refused this woman unless she accept the welfare board's scheme. (minutes of EBPW, August 1923, Edmonton City Archives, MC 213 C.1, file 11)

Other women who were active in the paid workforce were advised to change the nature of their work and to take on jobs that were more re-munerative – such as raising chickens and selling eggs (instead of sewing) – or to seek out long-term contracts (such as doing home laundry) rather than sporadic, informal jobs. Mrs B, for instance, was granted an allowance "but she is to be advised to undertake more practical work than manicuring if possible" (EBPW minutes, June 1923, Edmonton City Archives, MC 213 C.1, file11).

Mrs McC, a widow, was similarly in need of incentives. She claimed she was unable to work because of a leg injury that had incapacitated her, but the visiting social worker was of the opinion that she was de-liberately malingering. The board decided to force her into treatment, and presumably into a physical condition where she could take on paid work: "Woman incapable of any work owing to serious ulcerated condition of leg but refusing to accept medical treatment and hospital care. Committee considers that pressure should be brought to bear in the hopes of forcing woman to receive treatment" (report, March 1921, Edmonton City Archives, MS 213.C2, file 9).

Women were not the only ones to fall under medical scrutiny. A mother who applied for the allowance on the grounds that her husband was totally disabled was often told that the husband had to submit to a medical check to determine whether his condition was amenable to treatment. If it was, he had to be treated to the extent that would fit him for paid work. Such was the case with Mrs P, who claimed that her husband was disabled: "Committee agreed that it was undesirable that Mr P should be allowed to settle down to absolute inactivity and pauperism without some effort being made to fit him for work. The secretary was authorized to take up this matter with him and if necessary to make his acceptance of medical treatment a condition to further assistance" (minutes of advisory committee, February 1920, Edmonton City Archives, MS 213.C3, file 3).

Women were encouraged to take on paid work that the welfare board deemed rational and appropriate – indeed, they were coerced into doing so. Some women, however, went too far and were observed to be too thoroughly caught up in the role of worker outside the home, to the detriment of their primary responsibility to their children. The EBPW viewed with alarm reports that women receiving the allowance were not found at their homes during the day by visiting social workers, suggesting they were out earning money and leaving children unsupervised. Mrs M, for instance, was dropped from the rolls "until further investigation can be made and the woman can be seen in her own home. It is thought probable that the applicant earns money ... owing to the fact that she can never be found at home in the afternoons" (visiting committee minutes, 14 July 1919, Edmonton City Archives, MS 213.C.1, file 1).

Good Women

At the same time as recipients were expected to be active (but not too active) participants in the paid economy, they were also expected to uphold a particular gender ideal. Simply by requesting an allowance from the state, these women had fallen short of the ideal situation for a woman, which was to be a privatized dependant of a man who held legal responsibility and authority over her and their children. Women who weren't able to achieve that status could still be held to a version of it.

Women could fall short of this ideal in two main ways. The first was to be too close to a man or men, outside the framework of legal marriage; the second was to maintain too great a distance from a man in situations where a marriage might legally exist. Women who failed to manage an appropriate social distance from men in either of these ways could find themselves disqualified from state support.

In all the cases of women living in unacceptable proximity to men, never was the question raised as to whether the men were in fact providing financial support to the woman or her children. Simply having a male companion was enough to, in effect, cancel the implicit contract between the mother and the state, in which her complete investment in the work of mothering was exchanged for a pension. The board members debated what constituted "proof" of immoral cohabitation – Cooking for a man? Doing domestic chores? Being found in his home,

instead of the woman's own? – and bemoaned the lack of clear government directives for dealing with immoral women.

Much of the EBPW's time was taken up with cases of "immorality,"
where recipients were suspected of having a man around. These wom-
en refused to reprivatize their reproduction: they continued to accept
wages from the state, in the form of mothers' allowances, rather than
enter into privatized relations of formal dependency on men. The board
seems to have been under the impression that the Mothers' Allowance
Act prohibited women from having sexual relations with men to whom
they were not married, even though the act itself said nothing about
individual sexual conduct. In the case of Mrs B, for example, the board
"advises that under the Mothers' Allowance Act this woman's allowance shall cease owing to her proved immorality" (Report of the Board,
14 February 1921, Edmonton City Archives, MS 2131 C.1, file 9). Mrs V,
for example, was considered to have a suspiciously close relationship
with the men she boarded in her home. She was described in the board
minutes as a woman who

> has been maintaining children by outside work and by the aid of two male
> boarders. In the opinion of the probation officer the home conditions are
> unsatisfactory, the presence of one of these men having been objected to
> by the husband when he was at home. No more assistance should be ren-
> dered to this woman while she maintains these roomers, and she should
> be advised to this effect. In the event of her refusing to comply with these
> suggestions case to be handed to department of neglected children. (re-
> port of board, December 1920, Edmonton City Archives, MS 213.C.1, file 8)

Similarly, Mrs S, a widow with four children, had her allowance
stopped in 1921 "owing to the unsatisfactory conditions under which
she was keeping house for a man. Allowance was recommended after
she had moved into a home of her own, [s]he has now returned to the
man under the same conditions as before, and the committee considers
no further payments should be made" (report of board, May 1923MS
213.C.1, file 1). These allegations of immorality were levelled at women
who did not keep men away, and thus could be said to have violated
the implicit contract under which they received support through the
mothers' allowance program.

The second way in which women could violate this contract was by
keeping at a distance a man who, in the view of the state authorities
charged with administering the allowance, really ought to be in that

woman's household. In this version, any woman who could potentially have a husband support her was expected to have that husband support her.

Women who claimed to have been deserted by their husbands were subjected to scrutiny as to whether the man had really disappeared or whether the woman simply didn't want him around. The most vexing cases were those of women who claimed their husbands had deserted them. Deserted wives ranked lower in the hierarchy of deserving mothers than did widows or those whose husbands were provably disabled. The EBPW declared itself willing to "help widows with both hands, deserted wives with one hand, wives with able-bodied husbands with neither. A deserted wife must have a warrant issued for her husband's arrest before relief is given: who knows but that he is around the corner?" ("Origins of Organization," typescript, 24, Edmonton Archives, RG 24, box 1, file 1).The deserted wife's story could not be verified by a death certificate or a doctor's note, meaning that any assistance given to a mother who claimed she had been deserted risked implicating the municipality and the province in fraud.

The end of the First World War brought some demobilized soldiers back to their families, but others apparently disappeared, taking their salaries with them. These cases came to the attention of the EBPW beginning in 1918, when one member "raised the question of soldier wife desertion cases, for which there seem to be no adequate means of securing redress. The Board considered these cases as most urgent and deserving" (minutes, 8 July 1918, Edmonton City Archives, MS 213.C.1, file 6).

Because there was no death certificate or doctor's note, and no way of proving that they really had been abandoned, these women's claims were viewed as potentially suspect. According to Florence King, the long-serving secretary of the EBPW,

> the number of cases of wife desertion ... are on the increase, and it is one of the most difficult matters which the board has to deal with. It is hard to bring the absconding husband to book and it would improve the situation materially if these men could be caught and have the police deal with them. As it now stands, the deserting husbands get across the border or over the ocean and it is well nigh impossible to trace them. ("Wife Deserters Are Increasing, Says Miss King," *Edmonton Bulletin*, 14 February 1923, 6)

The attorney general, in response to a query about whether a deserted wife could claim an allowance, acknowledged that "the question of deserted wives has been a very vexed one both in this and other provinces as wherever provision has been made to provide an allowance for deserted wives it has always been followed by a great number of doubtful applications. In many cases husbands have deliberately deserted in order to throw the care of the family on the province" (letter, 12 June 1923, PAA 75.126 7646, Mothers' Allowance general file). The man's function, according to this view of gender and money, was solely to provide financial support. No other aspect of his character or his fitness as a spouse or father was relevant, as long as he could be found and persuaded to pay for the upbringing of his children.

The experience of Mrs H demonstrates these expectations of gender relations. Mrs H was married to a man who, according to her account, was a failing small business owner in Edmonton, harsh and stingy with his family, with a habit of disappearing for extended periods of time and leaving them penniless. Mrs H took the unusual step of appearing before the EBPW in person to describe her family's plight:

Mrs H appeared before the committee in person and told her story at considerable length, to the effect that her husband had neglected his duty to his family for some time past and that it was impossible to secure adequate support from him. He had been summoned [by police] yesterday for non-payment of wages of the girl he employed in the Alberta Avenue shop, and evidently expecting further action he had removed a machine from the shop at night ... She also said she had been threatened with an action by the landlord of the house for arrears in the rent and she had come to the board to ask for advice in the matters. ("Cases dealt with by visiting committee May 1917," MS 213 C.2, file 1)

The board was evidently moved by Mrs H's story, noting that "the case seemed to be a very difficult one, the woman representing her husband as unreasonable, impatient and harsh." Nonetheless, rather than being granted an allowance outright, Mrs H was "advised to ... make him see the seriousness of the situation [by allowing eviction proceeding to proceed] ... The idea of the committee was that the man should be brought face to face with his financial responsibility as fully and as forcibly as possible" (ibid.).

Mr H eventually abandoned the family completely, and his wife returned to ask for financial assistance, which was duly granted. However, after a few months he expressed (through means that have not survived) a desire to reconcile with his wife and return home. Mrs

H did not want him to return; for presumably good reason, she did not trust him to live up to his promises to start paying the rent and otherwise supporting the family. Nonetheless, the EBPW strongly advised her to take him back, and it set a limit on the amount of assistance she could expect to receive if she did not:

> After a careful consideration of the facts of this case, it was decide[d] to give the woman some temporary assistance but she should be given to understand that she must be willing to have the man return to her and assume support for the family as he had agreed to. She will be expected to give him a fair opportunity to make good on his promise and unless she accepts these conditions the board will not be disposed to give further assistance. (minutes of advisory committee, February 1918, Edmonton City Archives, MS 213 C.3, file 1)

No further record of any assistance to Mrs H exists.

Mrs H had been told she would not receive any allowance unless she agreed to live with a man; Mrs O was told she would not receive any if she did. Mrs O, a widow, had been claiming mothers' allowance when it was reported to a "lady visitor" that she was sharing her quarters with a man described as her fiancé. Mrs O was told to leave the man and that her allowance would continue only "as long as [she] refuses to live with man [sic] again until they can be legally married" (minutes of advisory committee, June 1920, Edmonton City Archives, MS 213 C.3, file 3). Mrs O evidently complied, as no further evidence of action by the EBPW to stop her allowance exists.

Both Mrs O and Mrs H appear to have preferred the mothers' allowance program – as capricious and invasive as it might have been – to dependence on an individual man. In the volatile and uncertain economic climate of early-twentieth-century Alberta, this may have been a very rational choice, given that flesh-and-blood men came with risks, from disability to desertion to bankruptcy; the province and the municipalities were more reliable, however straitened their economic circumstances. However, the gendered logic of the mothers' allowance program, coupled with concerns for cost containment at the provincial and municipal levels, did not make it easy for women to balance the risks of depending on a man. This gendered economic dilemma was articulated clearly by Mrs M in a letter she wrote to the provincial attorney general:

> I am a widow with four children and no means of keeping them, only the mothers' allowance which I receive. Now supposing I was to remarry

would the allowance be all stopped or would I still receive something to help raise and educate the children? Now perhaps you may think me independent, but I would rather remain as I am than have my children depend altogether on a stepfather however good he might be. (18 May 1922, PAA 75.126 7646, Mothers' allowance general file)

Readers will not be surprised that the province's response was that the allowance was payable only so long as Mrs M remained a widow without a connection to a man. Mothers might fall into circumstances in which their means of survival came from the state and not from a patriarchal marriage, but they were not to "think themselves independent" and opt out of dependence on a man, if such dependence was even a remote possibility.

Conclusion

In this chapter I have delineated a particular form of "baby trouble" in the course of which the existence of babies (or children) turned women into social and economic problems. Children were viewed as requiring the work of social reproduction if they were to be transformed into useful, productive citizens, and that work was almost invariably allocated to women. But this work required that resources be allocated, especially money, and that is where the crux of this particular "baby trouble" was to be found. As long as women did the work of social reproduction within the dyad of a patriarchal heterosexual marriage, the work was privatized and (relatively) unproblematic. The products of that labour, in the form of well-raised children, could benefit both their individual parents and the state that claimed them as citizens. But when that dyad broke apart, providing the resources for social reproduction fell not to individual men but to collective entities. The institutionalization of means for transferring these resources – such as the mothers' allowance scheme – created new relationships between women and the state, embodied in the municipal and provincial bureaucracies.

I contend that these relationships should be treated as both gendered and capitalist ones. Recent scholarship has been very attentive to the gendered dimension of the relationships established by welfare schemes, viewing them as extensions and bureaucratizations of patriarchy. This perspective is certainly applicable to Alberta – in the intensely gendered social, legal, and economic context of the young province, no relationships between women and men that involved the transfer of resources could be anything other than patriarchal. Canadian sociologists and social historians have also gone beyond simplistic gender analogies to more complex considerations of the relations between women and states.

I want to direct attention to the specifically productive and economic aspect of the relations activated by the Mothers' Allowance Act. At the municipal and provincial levels, the bureaucrats and civic leaders who oversaw the allowances clearly saw it as their business to oversee a particular type of labour from their clients, in order to ensure the production of a useful resource – healthy children who would grow up to be good adults.

Women in the program were thus held to standards reflecting both economic and gendered ideals. They were required to comport themselves in ways consistent with feminized norms in an asymmetrical gender order; in particular, they were to keep an appropriate social distance from men to whom they were not married (or the converse – to collapse the social distance between themselves and men to whom they were, or could be, married). They were also required to conform to the norms of efficiency and rationalization that characterized good workers and to allocate their time as productively as possible. The latter included balancing the work of child care, paid by the state, with other paid work that enabled them to reduce the state's childrearing costs.

The case files of the EBPW and related correspondence suggest that some mothers did not fall into line as either good women or good workers. They persisted in striking up alliances with inappropriate men, rejecting the husbands to whom they were legally bound, working too much or too little outside or inside their homes, and otherwise pushing the boundaries of the implicit gendered and economic contracts under which they received the allowances.

This "independent" behaviour on the part of women can be contextualized in the particular historic circumstances of the 1910s and 1920s, during which the dislocations of war, environmental crises, and economic volatility compelled women to press their claims of entitlement to support and led state bureaucracies to minimize, circumscribe, and regulate these claims. The "crisis tendencies" in gender relations that fuelled the struggle for suffrage and the Dower Act provided both the precedent and the rationalization for decoupling mothers from economic dependence on men. In this way, the existence of children was used to embed women in new relations with municipal and provincial governments.

6 Unless the Infant Lives, the National Gain Is Nil: Infant Mortality as Failed Reproduction

Introduction

This chapter develops themes introduced earlier regarding the function of reproduction in the social imaginary of early Alberta. I take up the arithmetic of reproduction, in the form of vital statistics, those numbers that represent changes in the size of a population. This chapter sets aside momentarily the concerns with gender that were the focus of the previous two chapters, to consider the meanings of human life itself in the social imaginary of early Alberta. Gender is not always centre stage here, but it is remains powerfully present, given that mothers rather than parents were figured as the producers of precious and endangered lives.

"Baby trouble," in this context, involved babies who had ceased to exist, as reflected in Alberta's birth and death statistics. Vital statistics record two types of change in a population: gain and loss (or increase and decrease). But not all gains carry the same political and symbolic valence, nor do all losses. The first (and as far as I can find, the only) use of the term "sociology of vital statistics," in an American academic journal, makes this quite clear. It is from the 1911 edition of *Journal of Home Economics*:

> The sociology of vital statistics is wonderfully fascinating to the student. In scarcely any other way can he gain so vivid a conception of the actualities of modern social life ... [How] enlightening is the tragedy of the death-rate. The student is appalled when he first comprehends the wanton sacrifice of human life, the reckless waste of our vital resources, through ignorance, disease, and bad social condition ... Gradually he

realizes that slaughter in war is not so deadly as institutional murder in times of peace ... Then he turns to the triumphs of scientific prevention, and takes new courage. To his amazement he learns that there is actually being achieved a conquest of death ... A single flash of knowledge enables him vividly to see how much the life of man lies in his own hand. (Elliott 1911, 38)

In this chapter I suggest that one form of vital event in particular – infant mortality – has been understood as an especially troubling and troubled occurrence. Infant mortality represents the near-simultaneous arrival through birth and departure through death of human life. Here I examine how temporal juxtaposition became understood as perverse and unnatural and was linked metaphorically to broader historical experiences of the body politic.

Many other scholars have explored the ways in which concerns about infant mortality have been used to justify launching or expanding state interventions ranging from mothercraft to eugenics. Most notably, Anna Davin (1978) and Ann Stoler and Frederick Cooper (1995) have launched many inquiries into the governance of infant health and maternal behaviour, all in the name of the state. In a slightly different vein, Lorna Weir (2006) has focused attention on perinatal mortality, or the constitution and extinction of a subject just before or immediately following birth, through close readings of legal struggles over the beginnings of life and death.

In this chapter I focus on anxieties that arise when the two ends of the lifespan are brought into abrupt proximity, when births are temporally proximate to their own negation by death. While many scholars have concentrated on the political and legal uses to which infant deaths have been put and the ways in which they have been used to mobilize public welfare programs, I am here interested in the saturation of infant mortality rates with meaning in the popular imagination by means of persistent tropes, even before the initiation of such programs.

Infant mortality represents thwarted reproduction. Those who should have lived have instead died, whether through misfortune, negligence, or deliberate intervention. The fact that this death occurs so soon after the beginning of life gives infant mortality a particular urgency as a social problem, because the death of an infant is more easily understood as an ethical crisis than the death of an older person, who has already experienced a full measure of life and whose death can be more easily understood as appropriate or natural.

As Weir (2006) has demonstrated, in the mid-twentieth century the perinatal boundaries of personhood were constructed out of contemporary anxieties about birth as a social problem, with particular types of perinatal deaths coming to be understood as especially problematic. Going back earlier, Bayat-Rizi (2008, 122) has described the emergence of a distinction between timely deaths from natural causes and "premature" or untimely deaths. Infant deaths are a prime example of "unnatural" mortality, given the temporal compression of life in cases of infant mortality, when death comes before full social life is attained. Anthropologists and sociologists have long talked of these circumstances where life and death are proximate as "liminal" states (see Kaufman and Morgan's 2005 review of the literature on the beginnings and endings of life); however, "liminal" does not seem as good a descriptor as "perverse." A birth that ends in rapid death is not a "real" birth, insofar as it does not augment the population but decreases it, because of life's unnaturally rapid appearance and disappearance. Perverse and unproductive births such as these confound the categorization of biological phenomena, in which death and life are distinct categories, separated by taxonomies that distinguish fertility and mortality.

The interwar period in Alberta is fruitful for this inquiry not only because it was a particularly stressful period, but also because birth rates and death rates, including infant mortality rates, were first compiled in 1919. Infant mortality rates denote a population that both exists and does not exist; they represent lives that have come into being and then quickly exited. But as we will see, this absent life continues to exist in representations of lost potential, of the assets that could have been fully present had they not been wasted because of the inability to keep infants alive.

Infant mortality – birth haunted by death – was rhetorically stylized through analogies to two specific collective traumas: the aftermath of the First World War, and the Great Depression, which in Alberta arrived even before the 1929 stock market crash. The stylization of "failed" births through metaphors of economic inefficiency and military defence is particular to Alberta's own history, just as, for example, the stylization of collective efforts to change infant mortality in Wilhelmine Germany as *kulturkampf*, or cultural struggle (Frohman 2006, 452), was tied to contemporary events.

In the archives, infant deaths are sometimes visible as events occurring at the level of the individual. For instance, in the case records kept by district nurses in the Glenbow Archives in Calgary, infant mortality is visible as specific babies undergoing specific traumas and deaths. Similarly, in the remembrances of adults from the early twentieth century, losses of children form part of the narrative of an individual life (Silverman 1998). In public discourse, however, the sentiment and the tragic affect that attended the loss of a particular child or mother was subsumed into a more collectivized loss, a waste of human potential instead of, or in addition to, a privatized tragedy. This depiction of infant mortality, without particularized sentiment or affect, served to diagnose the population: the failures and tragedies of the social body were read off the failures and tragedies of individuals.

In this chapter I rely heavily on reports from small-town papers, for several reasons. In the first part of the twentieth century, most papers were owned and run by town residents rather than by large conglomerates (Wetherell and Kmet 1995). Unlike the newspapers of the two major cities, Edmonton and Calgary, small-town papers concentrated on local and provincial news, and editorial boards made free use of the news sections and opinion pages to promote their own views. "Boilerplate" news, obtained from wire services and printed verbatim, occupied a smaller and smaller proportion of news sections until by the 1920s, the use of "boilerplate" had completely ended (Wetherell and Kmet 1995:67). The editors preferred to fill their pages with local and provincial news and – if local news was scant – opinion and commentary on local and provincial issues.

The papers, mainly weeklies, were also infused with the ethic that Wetherell (2005) calls "boosterism," in which the function of a newspaper was not so much to spread news as to promote the development of the town it served. "Boosterism" could take the form of unreflecting celebration of small-town life and commerce, but it also took the form of diagnosing and prescribing remedies for social problems that, once eradicated, would make Alberta a better place. Besides articles on infant mortality, local newspaper writers ran many pieces in which news shaded into opinion on topics such as the substitution of mixed ranching for farming, control of prostitution, flat-tax systems, dower laws, and Esperanto. The pieces on infant mortality thus formed part of a broader discourse regarding how to assess and correct the flaws of the "last best west."

Clearly, these sources do not represent all sentiment in Alberta at the time. The presses were owned by men (and a few women) of British descent who were, if not wealthy, at least well-off, and who had significant financial and moral capital invested in the idea of a modern, progressive Alberta. Attitudes towards those who fell outside this circle – the poor, the non-Anglo, the displaced First Nations – were for the most part predictably condescending and often demeaning. The courses of action recommended for such people – that they overcome their ignorance, follow experts' advice, educate themselves, and improve themselves generally – were also predictably paternalistic and individualized. These attitudes, though, are the backdrop to this chapter; they are not the focus of it.

Death and Infants in Alberta after the First World War

A tour of the social imaginary of infant mortality in Alberta might begin at the annual Baby Welfare Week held in Calgary, then the largest city in Alberta, in the early interwar period. The Baby Welfare Weeks consisted of exhibits, speakers, and films on the latest "scientific" advances in child development, and attendees received a detailed booklet containing program notes and other useful short articles. The intended audience was mothers and mothers-to-be in Calgary and the surrounding area, and the week's activities were organized by the municipal health authorities and sponsored by commercial enterprises whose profits depended on convincing mothers that their infants' lives were at risk.

The programs for the week's events made it clear that infant mortality was an ever-present danger to families and to the greater polities in which families were embedded and that infant survival was tied to the state's military and economic capacities. In 1917 the week's theme was "Our Empire Builders," as was proclaimed on the cover of the program, echoing Davin's (1978) evocation of "imperial motherhood" in the United Kingdom. On the inside, readers were asked, "Do you know that intelligent motherhood conserves the Nation's best crop? A low infant mortality rate indicates high community intelligence? Health first is a form of safety first?" (Glenbow M8401–35). The 1923 program reminded women that "the race marches forward on the feet of little children" (ibid.).

These exhortations from civic authorities evoked a progressive vision of a nation dependent on a constant increase in safe and healthy babies. Meanwhile, the advertisements from local merchants conjured up the converse of infant survival. In these ads, the spectacle of infant mortality was repeatedly invoked, with some advertisers stating explicitly that their product was necessary to prevent infant life from being snuffed out. One merchandiser in 1918 whose store sold "combs, baby trusses,

6.1 Using infant mortality to sell castor oil. The advertisement in the lower right corner reads in part: "Infant mortality in ages past has been something frightful, something almost beyond belief. And even today it occupies the time and the mind of leading physicians in all countries. The death rate among infants is being gradually reduced through new methods of hygiene, new preventatives and new remedies for infants."

Source: *Chinook Advance*, 14 July 1921, 3

rubber bibs, etc." informed readers that "your baby's life depends on these precautions" (ibid.). Other advertisers reminded readers that the early days were the most dangerous ones and that if mothers did not use vitamins, sterilizers, and other specialized items, they might lose their infants.

The contrast between the optimistic possibilities of enhanced infant survival and the implicit pessimism of the ads typifies the representation of infant mortality in the early twentieth century. The infant population of Alberta was framed as simultaneously precious to both parents and the province, and as threatened.

Before the First World War, there was no infant mortality rate as such in Alberta, as no figures on infant births and deaths were collected. The 1914–18 war and its loss of life carved the contours for public concern about infant mortality. Although the age-specific quantification of death had been possible in the English-speaking world since the seventeenth-century "political arithmetic" of John Graunt (Bayat-Rizi 2008, 127), the treatment of infant mortality as not only an individual tragedy but also a problem of politics in Alberta began in the postwar period, somewhat later than elsewhere. Across Canada, statistics on infant births and deaths (along with other vital rates) were first compiled in 1919, as was the case in other British colonies and dominions such as Australia, New Zealand, and South Africa, where population-level mortality phenomena, especially infant mortality, were quantified in the wake of the war (McPhail 1927, 476).

The impact of the war on concerns about infant mortality was also noted in countries where quantification had existed for years. Richard Titmuss (1943) summarized changes in Great Britain's infant mortality patterns, attributing state awareness of and intervention in infant mortality to the shock experienced by the country in the wake of war. "There is perhaps something rather shocking," Titmuss wrote, "in the idea that it took a war to focus public attention on a wastefully high infant death rate" (12). Titmuss linked infant survival with military fitness and argued that the former would not be properly attended to "unless the threat of mass devastation was upon us" (13). In fact, declines in infant mortality had begun well before the First World War (and even before the Boer War, which had also occasioned such hand-wringing), but the link between war and infant mortality was now established in the public imagination (Woods, Patterson, and Woodward 2010).

Anna Davin (1978) provides extensive analysis of the programs to save babies by improving mothers, in the name of the empire. These programs sprang up across Britain at the beginning of the twentieth century. With regard to Ontario and central Canada, Mariana Valverde (2008), Catherine Arnup (1994), and Cynthia Comacchio (1993) chronicled similar projects for the moral uplift of mothers, fuelled by the newfound "sciences" of mothercraft and domestic economy and embedded in the broader context of the Social Gospel movement around the same time.

On the far side of the prairies, however, events moved more slowly. In Alberta, it was not until after the First World War that "child-saving" – a broad term that included moral rehabilitation as well as the physical preservation of children – gathered momentum as a social movement. In 1918 the provincial Superintendent of Neglected Children reported that "with almost unprecedented rapidity, social organizations have been organizing child welfare departments, baby clinics, and other child-saving activities ... [and] arousing people to the realization of startling facts concerning unnecessary infant mortality" ("Superintendent of Neglected Children Annual Report 1918," 9, Galt Archives). A contemporary editorial in the *Claresholm Review-Advertiser* connected the war with heightened awareness of human stock as wealth and security for the nation: "With all its horrors, suffering and losses, the Great War conferred at least one benefit to mankind in that it opened the eyes of all the people, and particularly all the governments ... [to the fact that] the greatest of all national assets are people" ("More about this wonderful age," 25 June 1926, 2).

Managing Population in Alberta

Under the UFA, calls to improve the population led to several social programs, the most notorious of which entailed sterilizing people considered unfit to reproduce for genetic or social reasons. Xenophobia towards non-Anglo-Saxon immigrants was also pronounced among many members of the UFA.

Xenophobia and calls for sterilization are partly rooted in anxieties about population. As a population phenomenon, infant mortality is distinct from either of these, for it involves the net loss of people who already exist – that is, the shrinking of an already existing population rather than the shaping of a future one. In Alberta, sterilization and xenophobia focused on preventing new and presumably undesirable people from entering the population, rather than the loss of already valued people. The children who were lost to infant mortality – the objects of contemplation in the anxious discussion about what must be done – were clearly imagined as precious and important, as economic and political assets to Alberta, not as potential dangers, as was the case with the imaginary children whom the eugenically sterilized might have borne, or the "undesirable" immigrants who might have flooded into Alberta had they not been stopped.

This particular characteristic of infant mortality as a social problem – the concern about the loss of new citizens rather than the prevention of future citizens – distinguished it from Alberta's other forays into population governance, in the form of eugenics and immigration control. The lost infants, potential new citizens now irretrievably gone, had been allowed to die when they should have lived. The framing of infant mortality as failure resonated throughout public discussions of health, reproduction, and population growth.

Natural and Unnatural Increase

Concerns about infant mortality in Alberta were first and foremost concerns about population growth. Increasing population was considered an intrinsic good, but not all forms of population growth were equally desirable. Population growth through a continued excess of births over deaths – "natural increase" – was preferred to, and contrasted with, population growth from already born people coming to Alberta via immigration. Natural increase was associated with the expansion of established pioneer stock, whereas immigration entailed perceived concerns about how to assimilate new Albertans who were not white or English-speaking. A verbose editorialist for the *Lethbridge Herald*, commenting on the release of vital statistics for 1919 – the first year that such information existed – linked infant mortality not only to the growth and perpetuation of cities and provinces, and of Canada as a nation, but also to the most desirable way of perpetuating those political units. Both the quantity and the quality of population growth were implicated in birth rates and infant deaths. Infant mortality represented a lost opportunity for Canada to grow "from within," through biological replenishment, rather than "from without," by taking in immigrants:

If there is anything to be gleaned from the vital statistics of the year gone by, it may be found that too great a ratio of mortality of infants under five years to the death roll in the city. It serves to show that the campaign of child welfare in its particular relation to infants is one that is abundantly time-worthy and of great importance, if we are to rely on the increase of our population of native Canadians more than on immigration. Of the two, the former is of greater importance in that the principle of growing from within is preferable to growing from without. (editorial, "Infant mortality in the city," 5 January 1920)

The lost children had been part of Alberta, coming from "within," as distinct from the alien immigrants from "without." An editorialist for the *Irma Times* commended the new UFA government for identifying infant mortality as a political problem linked to immigration. The "vacancies" created by infant deaths, he argued, would be filled up by immigrants, and as a consequence, foreigners would substitute for true Albertans:

> The new minister of health … is on the right track in endeavoring to improve the province's life and death numbers. In an address in Calgary a few days ago he called attention to the too-high infant mortality rate … urging upon the public the seriousness and needlessness of this annual loss. It would be better, he very rightly claimed, to conserve the life we have here now than to keep on filling up unnecessary vacancies by immigration. ("Save the people," 7 October 1921, 5)

Two years later, the same newspaper (and possibly the same editorialist) reiterated that

> of the many natural resources which the prairie provinces possess, the greatest is their people. The natural increase from births is Canada's best source of population and the growth and maintenance of this increase is her first duty. ("Natural resources bulletin," 30 November 1923, 7)

Because of this compelling political duty, continued the editorial, "there is considerable satisfaction to be gained from the fact that the infant mortality rate was less than that of the preceding year" (ibid.).

Mortality Rates and Numbers

In the interwar years, representations of the infant mortality rate tended to be highest in public settings where convincing rhetoric was required. For instance, in an address to the Alberta Women's Institute annual meeting in 1916, Irene Parlby claimed that "the high death rate among infants in Alberta is something like 35 per cent … It [is] high time the women of the province took steps to remedy this" (*Grain Growers' Guide*, 18 March 1916, 29). The *Bassano Mail* reported that Alberta's infant mortality in 1926 was 77.2 per thousand, down from 89.5 in 1925 ("Infant mortality decreasing," 29 December 1927, 2). However in a 1928 address to the UFWA, a Mrs J.W. Field reported infant mortality as 85 per thousand (*The UFA*, 1 February 1928, 28). Setting aside these variances, the reported rate was always described as too high, and as dangerous and unnatural. The Alberta government's failures to safeguard its resources were compared unfavourably to the successes of Alberta's closest peers within the empire, especially New Zealand and Australia.

These concerns about infant mortality were profoundly gendered. Infants were represented only in conjunction with mothers, who were assigned the most direct responsibility for keeping new life from dying too soon. I did not find a single reference to fathers as either causes of or bulwarks against infant mortality. Infant mortality was represented as a concern for every Albertan because of its implications for the health of the population, but it was the female half of that population – actual and potential mothers – who were viewed as responsible for improving the infant mortality figures. The responsibility placed on mothers was great – besides shouldering a broader duty to raise good citizens, they were responsible for the very existence of the country, by keeping babies alive.

Neither the security nor the economy of Alberta could be ensured as long as the mortality rate stayed high. As long as so many infants were being allowed to die, Alberta's claim to be a true modern polity was in jeopardy. As a speaker at the 1918 Lethbridge Child Welfare Week put it, "we are not in a position to be a democracy when we waste more than 30,000 children annually, and the ability of a nation shows up in making itself strong [*sic*] to withstand tyranny" (*Lethbridge Herald*, 3 May 1918, 8; see also "Slaughter of the Innocents," *Chinook Advance*, 22 May 1924, 6). A feature in the *Empress Express* titled "Judge nation by child death rate" (13 May 1930, 5) made the case that "infanted [*sic*] mortality [is] an index of any civilization."

A few commentators described infant mortality in moral or affective terms. A writer for the *Carbon News* referred to the "slaughter of the innocents" ("Take care of the babies," 27 January 1921), but even this reference was framed by the qualification that "apart from the human aspect in the unwarranted loss of child life ... [the most important aspect] is the loss to the state itself" (ibid.). More typical was the line of argument in the *Claresholm Review-Advertiser* that "the waste of infant life affects not only the happiness of the home, but the well-being of the nation" ("The greatest waste of human life," 20 August 1918, 8). In this commentary, the well-being of the nation received much more attention, and many more superlatives, than the comparatively bland "happiness of the home." There was little sentimentality here regarding the figure of the child; instead, infants were construed as part of a greater social machine, and infant mortality as a threat to that machine.

The rhetoric surrounding infant mortality was dominated by two metaphors: collective defence and economic growth. The babies who had gone missing through excess mortality were imagined primarily as soldiers missing from some future army, and secondarily as economic resources wasted and inefficiently dispersed. Humanitarian presentations of the tragedy of child death and depictions of individual suffering were few compared to analogies to military strength, national defence, investment, and efficiency. Infant mortality was thus figured as both excess and lack – as too much death and too little strength.

Military Metaphors

In discussions of infant mortality, metaphors of military strength (or lack thereof) were more plentiful than those of economic growth. One editorialist pointed to Great Britain, the "mother country" for the socially dominant ethnic groups in Alberta, as an example of what could happen when countries failed to protect their infants, by invoking troop strength during the First World War: "Great Britain now realizes that the neglect of her babies during the years 1872 to 1899 cost her the lives of 1,600,000 male infants alone who would have been of military age today if they had been spared – a priceless reservoir of manpower wasted" ("The greatest waste of human life," *Claresholm Review-Advertiser*, 30 August 1918, 8).

In her regular radio series, Maude Riley of the Calgary Child Welfare Association, a suffragist and well-known "modern" progressive activist, told listeners that

> the question [of infant mortality] is one of dire necessity and will have to be dealt with by our provincial and federal governments ... 15,000 babies that might be saved die in Canada every year. Think of it, more babies died every year than there were men killed overseas [in the First World War]. We blame the greater slaughter of men during the Great War to [*sic*]

the German autocracy. Then can we not justly blame the appalling casualty rate among babies to our own apathetic indifference? (*The Albertan*, June 1916, PAA M466-4)

In case listeners missed the point, Riley titled her lecture "The Greatest Patriotism Is Interest in [the] Child" (ibid.). In a speech the following year to a city conference on child welfare, Riley linked the loss of new life to the perceived underpopulation of the West: "If every child who had died had lived, there would be a number great enough to duplicate the present population of our western cities" ("Baby welfare sessions brought to close with interesting address," *Calgary Herald*, 6 May 1918, PAA M466-4).

The following year, the Alberta Women's Institute adopted "Save the Babies" as its slogan and launched a series of measures intended to protect against the wastage of precious Albertan life. These included campaigns for the mandatory pasteurization of milk, for more post-partum check-ups for infants, and for better education of new and prospective mothers on how to keep their babies alive through proper hygiene, sanitation, and breastfeeding. In the AWI's annual bulletin, members read that

> the Institute, owing to the high infant mortality rate, intends to launch an active campaign of conserving the baby life of Alberta. It is estimated that two out of every seven deaths in this province today are babies under one year. The Alberta soldier in the trench has seven chances to live to the Alberta baby's one. The hardest job in Alberta is being a baby. (McGregor 1917, 31)

The *Redcliff Review* also compared infant mortality to the deaths of soldiers:

> Canada sacrifices 30,000 little babes under one year of age every year! Somebody said about the close of the war that the trenches in Flanders and France were a safer place for Canadian life than the cradles of Canada! (12 June 1924, 5)

So did the *Chinook Advance*:

> Canada lost 10,000 of her fine young men in the Great War. She loses 20,000 of her little babes every year in peace and war alike ... Can you say as the

preacher did of old over the little graves "the Lord has given and the Lord has taken away, blessed be the name of the Lord"? Assuredly not ... We shall have to say "cursed be the name of the city or community. (22 May 1924, 6)

In Calgary, Maude Riley and her Child Welfare Association pushed local leaders towards an understanding of babies as precious, endangered, and of great importance to collective well-being. Riley, in an exasperated letter to a Calgary mayor whom she perceived as insufficiently supportive of setting up a new clinic for infants, wrote that

the aim of this clinic is not curative but prevention ... When you think that almost as many babies die in Canada every year as there were men killed and died overseas in the whole Canadian army over the whole four years of the Great War, it is no wonder that this question is [of] such paramount importance to the state. (21 August 1922, Glenbow M8401-28)

Economic Metaphors

Infant mortality was also represented as wastage of the "best source of population growth," expressed through Fordist metaphors of inefficiency and non-productivity:

One of the great and impelling duties of this generation is to provide adequate protection or the citizens of tomorrow, who are the babes of today. We need an awakening to the importance of the child as the primary asset of the nation. The waste of infant life affects not only the happiness of the home, but the well-being and the future of the nation ... There is no loss so irretrievable as the wastage of these human resources. *There is no economy so fundamental and no investment comparable to that devoted to the conservation and all-round development of infant life.* We must save the lives ... [of] a healthy, intelligent and moral generation of young Canadians equipped for the tremendous nation-building tasks that await them ("Child Welfare Program of the Alberta Social Service League," *Red Deer Advocate*, 11 September 1918, 2; emphasis added)

The replenishment and expansion of the population through children was explicitly likened to other forms of accumulation. In its *Blue Book for 1917*, an anonymous member of the Alberta Women's Club wrote that a low and decreasing rate of infant mortality marks the attainment of a high degree of civilization. The growth of population *like other forms of wealth* results not only from increases in gains but also from diminution of losses, the excess of births over deaths being enlarged by a rise in the birth rate but perhaps also more by a fall in the [infant] death rate ... About one-ninth of the deaths in this province during the last few years have been among infants less than a year old. In the joy that heralds the birth of a babe, there should also be great care lest the life thus begin be ended too soon. Unless the infant lives, the national gain is nil. (1917, 53; emphasis added)

Another contributor likened the prevention of infant mortality to investment, in that the national wealth depended on salvaging rather than wasting the "capital" represented by infants: "To save our infants for future citizens is a salvage policy of national importance ... Infants become assets to the country. Here is abundant need for a wise policy of conservation" (editorial, "Infant mortality in the city," 5 January 1920). In several instances, infants were depicted as potential sources of wealth just like Alberta's mineral and agricultural stocks. The *Irma Times*, in a series titled "Natural Resources Bulletin," included a piece on infant mortality (20 November 1923), noting with approval that it was decreasing. It was sandwiched between a series instalment on mineral ores and an instalment on the pulpwood industry. An article in the *Redcliff Review* went even further with the comparison, likening infants to raw, unprocessed resources as distinct from finished ones:

The greatest of all the natural resources of Canada is her children ... The automobile, aeroplane and radio are only machines, whereas children are the future of the state. In order to preserve and develop in the highest degree the great resources represented by child life [new health measures must be taken] ... Can Canada afford to lose 514 mothers and babies every week? [Information about child health] is needed in order to bring home to the people the greatness of this national resource, and how it might be preserved. ("Welfare of our children is question of vital concern to the people of Canada," 27 November 1924, 3)

Responses to Infant Mortality

Over the course of the interwar years, the infant mortality rate in most of Canada dropped gradually. The rate for Canada as a whole was estimated at 34.3 deaths per thousand live births in 1921, falling to 28.6 in 1938 (Statistics Canada 1976).

The pattern in Alberta, however, appears to have been different. Infant mortality figures were given as significantly higher than the national average. The chart below shows the number of deaths of children under one year of age per thousand live births in the southern city of Lethbridge during the 1920s, according to the city's health department. The numbers are surprisingly high, but it is worth remembering that not all births may have been registered with the city and that not all infant deaths would have occurred to babies who were born in the same city in the same year.

The trends in Lethbridge are consistent with spot estimates from other places such as Edmonton, in which estimates of the infant mortality rate varied between 50 and 120 per thousand. The causes of death included infectious disease, malnutrition, and "conditions present at birth," the latter category a catch-all for obstetric crises and neonatal fatalities, accounting for between 40 and 48 per cent of deaths of children under the age of one year (Corbett 1979, 11). However, the baby-saving efforts launched in Alberta to try to bring down these rates were concentrated not on the conditions into which Albertan babies were born, but on the knowledge and skills of mothers, who presumably would be able to effect great savings in child lives if they were properly trained in the care of babies.

The infant death rate was addressed by a range of public and private initiatives. On the public side, the UFA, pressed hard by its women's wing, the UFWA, created a unified provincial board of health, provided subsidies to municipal hospitals to deal with the eternal complaints about the costs of maternal and child health care, and established travelling baby clinics, staffed by public health nurses, who diagnosed and treated sick children at no cost (Corbett 1979). Other initiatives came from philanthropic and social welfare organizations, often in partnership with municipal or provincial governments, and focused on teaching mothers how to care for very young children.

In Lethbridge, for example, in 1918 the local nursing mission established a free milk station to provide cow's milk for women who might otherwise have fed their weaned children on water, and "to see that the babies were doing well and advising the mothers where necessary re feeding and general care with the result that during the hot months of last summer, our list of sick babies was practically nil and out of the 110 maternity cases only 2 normal babies have died" ("Annual Report

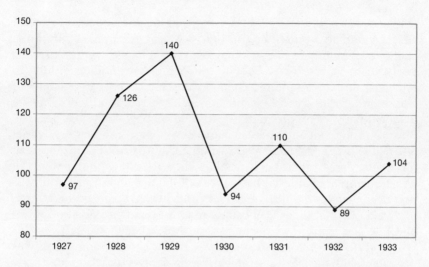

6.2 Deaths under one year of age per 1,000 live births, Lethbridge Department of Health.

Source: Lethbridge Department of Health Annual Reports, Glenbow Archives

of Lethbridge Nursing Mission, 16 May 1918," Galt Archives). The Lethbridge City Council also sponsored Baby Welfare Week, during which experts from larger cities such as Calgary and Regina addressed mothers regarding the preservation of infant life and babies were registered, charted, and measured. The program for the 1921 Baby Welfare Week declared that "every mother in Lethbridge should make an effort to attend these sessions, even at the cost of neglecting that most important event, spring cleaning. By all means have the baby charted and weighed" (Lethbridge Nursing Mission, Minutes 1916–21, Galt Archives). Out of ninety babies presented for examination during the 1918 Baby Week, six were deemed to be in danger and were admitted to the hospital for additional feeding (ibid.).

Larger urban centres such as Calgary took to the work of baby-saving with even greater zeal. Calgary held a National Baby Week events throughout the 1920s, at which mothers presented their infants for examination. They could even enter them in "best baby" contests, while taking in educational talks and demonstrations of techniques such as sterilizing milk bottles and concocting nutritious weaning foods. The success of these demonstration babies was tied to Alberta's prominence among nations; the 1926 Baby week program declared that "Alberta has reason to be proud of its children. It was an Alberta baby from the child welfare clinic in Calgary that last year obtained the first prize as the [British] Empire's best baby at the Wembley exhibition in July [in England], and it was another Alberta baby from a clinic at Redcliff that was awarded the second prize at the same exhibition in 1925" (1926 National Baby Week program, M840–35, Glenbow Archives). The trophy itself could not be displayed at the 1926 events, for it was in Nigeria, where it was being used to inspire mothers in that part of the empire to take better care of their babies. Babies from Alberta won the Shield of Merit during the National Baby Week of the British Empire Competition three times in the 1920s and 1930s and received "certificates of merit" five additional times ("A Tribute to Our Founders, Alberta Council on Child and Family Welfare 1977–1983, M667, Glenbow Archives).

The advice given to mothers at these public baby-saving events was consistent with the latest scientific thinking. Women who attended baby weeks in Alberta cities would have learned that their infants required supervised play in the sunshine, that they should breastfeed as long as possible, and that patent medicines should not be overused. One exhibit at Edmonton's Baby Week in 1918 depicted foods that were "baby's friends," including milk, sugar, fine wheat porridge, an orange, macaroons, cooked prunes, and cooked rhubarb; and those that were "baby's foes," such as meat, cheese, cabbage, bananas, pie, pickles, cake, and candy ("Child Welfare Institute Baby Clinic Opened," *Edmonton Bulletin*, 26 June 1918, 3).

Mothers were not the only ones targeted as responsible for the survival of infants. Social welfare activists such as Maude Riley called for scientific education for young girls before they became mothers, so that they would learn everything from proper dental care of infant teeth to modification of infant feeding (untitled speech, probably 1922, M8401, file 28, Glenbow Archives). There is no evidence that the "Little Mothers' Leagues" that Riley dreamed of ever came to pass, but her concern with training good future mothers was echoed in the UFWA's and other women's associations' calls for home hygiene and child studies to be introduced into school courses for girls.

While much attention was focused on properly training mothers, fathers (or men of any sort) were absent from the landscape of child saving, except as experts who gave lectures on child nutrition or in their public capacity as "town fathers." Male politicians were most notably involved in child saving through their work on the pasteurization of milk. This measure was promoted heavily by women's organizations, especially in the hot summer months when unrefrigerated and unpasteurized milk led to gastrointestinal upsets, diarrhea, and sometimes death. The work of standardizing city dairies to protect infants was a particular concern of Calgary's officer of medical health, Dr Cecil Mahood, who in the late 1910s organized meetings of concerned citizens (largely although not entirely men) to mobilize public opinion and put pressure on the city council to regulate milk sellers ("More than one thousand lives saved annually by Alberta health services," *Calgary Herald*, 17 February 1934, 3). His work was taken up and debated in other cities as councillors considered whether the possible savings in infant lives justified the expenditure of city funds for compliance ("Quality of city milk subject of much discussion by safety and health committee," *Edmonton Bulletin*, 20 May 1921, 1). Infant mortality was a powerful rhetorical concern, replete with emotionally laden images and metaphors, but when it came to putting scarce financial resources into public programs to prevent infant deaths, politicians balked. It was more politically palatable, and cheaper, to exhort mothers to take better care of their babies and to privatize responsibility for infant health.

Conclusion

Infant mortality was the most extreme form of "baby trouble" in early Alberta as well as the least concrete. The babies who troubled the collective imaginary did not exist; rather, they were the children (and the prospective citizens) who might have existed had it not been for social follies and errors. In this chapter I have argued that infant mortality is uniquely troubling in that it temporally fuses birth and death, creating, in the collective imagination, a spectral collection of those who might have (and should have) lived and added to the population, had they not been deprived of life unnaturally soon. Infant mortality also interpellates infants as innocents, deprived of the life that should have been theirs. In terms of vital statistics, infant mortality is the shadow side of the birth rate, representing failed reproduction. This failed reproduction is distinct from "normal" or "natural" mortality, in which the beginnings and endings of life are not juxtaposed so jarringly. Infant mortality is thus a goad to biopolitical management, an obvious target for those seeking to create a more rationalized, ordered population.

The preceding paragraph might be read as a general statement about infant mortality. However, the ways in which infant mortality is imagined and figured in popular discourse are contingent on historic experience and contexts. In some contexts, infant mortality might be considered unremarkable, a sad facet of human existence but not one that imposes a duty of outrage or mobilization on the communities in which it occurs (cf. Scheper-Hughes 1993). In Alberta, however, the collective traumas of the First World War, followed by drought, depopulation, and economic depression, provided the metaphors for infant mortality and for why it mattered so much to the emergent population. Infant mortality was not seen as inevitable; it was understood as something that could have and should have been otherwise. However, the concern with infant mortality and the assertions that something needed to be done were not founded solely on ethical concerns for the well-being of infants.

These spectral infants lost to unnatural mortality were imagined as soldiers who might have made up a future army and as economic assets that might have provided value and profit. Infant mortality itself was portrayed as losses in battle and as the inefficient wastage of resources – images that must have resonated with the newspaper-buying audience. In a province already grappling with anxieties over the quality and quantity of the population, and resorting to eugenic sterilization and xenophobic immigration restrictions, concern for preserving the lives of infants was consistent with ongoing political projects, which were not necessarily based on concern for individual well-being or for the equal value of all human lives.

7 Conclusion

The determining factor in history is, in the final instance, the production and reproduction of immediate life. This, again, is of a twofold character: on the one side, the production of the means of existence, of food, clothing and shelter and the tools necessary for that production; on the other side, the production of human beings themselves, the propagation of the species.

(Engels 1972, 71–2)

The nation's future depends on healthy babies!
(ad for Mrs Winslow's soothing syrup, *Drumheller Mail*, 13 April 1916)

When first the great Creator formed the skies
He made the seas and all that in them lies
Then hemispheres, but ere he gave his name,
He waved his hand, and lo! The Last West came.
...
The Last West aye! A gladdening welcome sent
To all who lived and labored in content ...
As with one heart those sturdy pioneers
Builded their dwellings for the coming years.
Developing in riches, beauty, grace.
To Progress they have started on the race.
What is their future? Oh that we could look
Into its depths as in a magic book
And know that ever in the coming years
No sad disaster on its page appears.
("The Last West," *Wetaskiwin Times*, 14 November 1907, 7)

Friedrich Engels and the anonymous copy writer for Mrs Winslow's Soothing Syrup agree: making new people is central to the work of building a society. The poet who invoked the glory of the "Last West" also addresses the building of a society, painting a picture of an Alberta marching boldly into the future, moving forward with speed and assurance towards a bright tomorrow. However, as we have seen, the work of making new people brings out tensions, contradictions, and states of crisis that complicate the organization of any society. In this light, the "Last West" author sounds like a cockeyed optimist, considering the many crises of reproduction that buffeted Alberta in the decades following the publication of this poem – maternal mortality, infant deaths, eugenic sterilization, abandoned mothers, illegitimacy, and so forth.

Why was it so challenging and so difficult to make new people? In this book I have recounted episodes in the imaginative economy of reproduction in Alberta, all of which partook of crisis, failure, or emergency. In this conclusion I discuss why reproduction is so continually vexed.

The fundamental reason for baby trouble is that the social relations that organize reproduction are decisively asymmetrical. Reproduction is treated as the moral terrain of women, as the contested responsibility of men (individually and collectively), and as a precarious necessity for the state. Power, legitimacy, and responsibility are distributed unevenly across these three entities, distorting the social imaginary of reproduction. This social imaginary has consequences for the distribution of resources, producing what I have termed an imaginative economy of reproduction, one that orders the allocation of money, status, material goods, and symbolic value.

Gender is powerful here. The making of children also requires the making of mothers as particular kinds of human beings. Many of the preceding chapters have foregrounded this invention of women as moral entities, based on their capacity as reproducers. In chapter 2, women were imagined as heroic martyrs, sacrificing themselves, through childbearing, for the greater good of the province. In chapters 3 and 5, dealing with the Beulah Home and the institution of mothers' allowances, (some) mothers were hallowed as noble figures through their relations with their children, doing the sanctified work of motherhood despite trials and tribulations. (At the same time, of course, other women were disdained as immoral and unworthy because they did not occupy the terrain of reproduction in morally legible or adequately sacrificial ways.) From this position of motherhood, women were able to make moral claims on individual men and male-dominated institutions, drawing on a shared repertoire of powerful images depicting maternal virtue.

Childbearing may have turned women into moral agents, but it also turned them into problems. Just as women produced babies, babies produced women – some valorized and elevated, others disregarded and made abject through the creation of new people outside the heterosexual marital dyad. These categories of good women and bad women were not always fixed, however – as we saw in chapters 3 and 4, "fallen women" at the Beulah Home could be redeemed and reinvested with value, and women whose alleged mental deficits made them unfit to reproduce, in the view of eugenic campaigners, could be returned to social life if they were rendered safe and harmless through sterilization.

In the patriarchal world of early Alberta, in which women had very limited control over or access to economic resources, the central dynamic in the imaginative economy of reproduction was the work of trying to move scarce resources from men to women – work that was legitimated and justified by the exigencies of reproduction. In this book we have seen efforts to secure money and political support for attended childbirth, for the sustenance of abject unwed mothers, for sexual sterilization for "inappropriate reproducers," and for women whose men refused to support them or were unable to do so. None of these claims were uncontested; all had to be fought within social institutions in which men, as a group, held the upper hand. Individual men were sometimes supportive of and involved in the work of reproduction; other times, they could and did exercise the option to discard their responsibilities.

However great were men's discursive contributions to the moral valorizing of heroic mothers, as a group they proved remarkably resistant to the prospect of actually supporting these mothers. In early Alberta, reproduction was ultimately an individualized and feminized responsibility, and there was considerable resistance to any attempts to collectivize it. In the annals of baby trouble, individual men are unfortunately most noticeable in their absence. This does not mean, of course, that all or even most men shied away from responsibilities for children. However, the most common forms of trouble occasioned by reproduction were the result of men's ability to context, evade, or simply absent themselves from the consequences of making babies.

Even while the costs and burdens of responsibility were downloaded onto women, the babies they produced were recognized as both precious and endangered by the emergent Alberta state and its institutions. The omnipresent metaphors of mothers as efficient producers and as valiant soldiers testify to the centrality of making new people in the imagination of Alberta. The sentimental glow that infuses maternity in other places and at other times paled beside the explicit and straight-forward equation of mothers with workers and fighters. The producer and the warrior carry out essential functions for any state, and these were ascribed via analogy to the mothers of Alberta. Their work was valuable even if they themselves had to struggle for the resources to carry it out. The precious services that mothers performed for the state were especially valorized when inflected with xenophobia and racism; biological reproduction by white Anglo-Saxon women was contrasted with the less desirable ways of filling up Alberta – through immigration by people who were not of the "right stock," or through the reproductive behaviour of the so-called "feeble-minded."

Mother-workers and mother-soldiers did the work of the state, but this work was dangerous. The precious babies could fall victim to infant mortality, or their mothers could die in childbirth. These losses were not just individual tragedies – they were crises for a polity founded on dreams of endless advancement, even as those dreams ran aground on the repeated crises of the early twentieth century. Even if the survival of the babies and mothers could be enhanced, women might be disinclined to produce those babies if the conditions were unfavourable. "Baby trouble," in all its variants, vexed the successive governments of early Alberta.

The foregoing analysis, like the rest of this book, is strongly rooted in feminist thought. Yet simple gender analysis, in which the primary social categories are masculinity and femininity, is not entirely sufficient to explain why baby trouble was so vexing. Women and men were clearly not homogenous groups – both were riven by class and wealth, especially as the difficult decades of the 1910s and 1920s wore on, and by ethnic distinctions between the white, Protestant, northern European settlers and everyone else.

In addition to the splits and tensions within these gender categories, other social categories and imaginations were brought to bear on baby trouble. While heterosexual patriarchy was unquestionably the dominant organizing framework for relations between men and women, other visions of social relations also shaped the way reproduction was imagined. For example, the distinction between the productive and the unproductive was as salient to the organization of mothers' allowances as were ideas about the proper gendered roles of women and men. The imagination of a Christian world of reproduction, in which the most

salient distinction is between the fallen and those in the midst of salvation, animated the work of Beulah at least as much as did notions
about proper masculinity or femininity. Similarly, ideas about science
and modernity drove debates about obstetric care, infant deaths, and
eugenic sterilization. None of these debates were ungendered, but none
were entirely *about* gender, either – a truth that is easy to overlook when
one is studying a biological process that is so inherently sex-divided.

I draw these general conclusions from studying early Alberta, but I
do not wish to overstate the generalizability of the Alberta case. This
was the "Last Best West," the economic and political frontier of Canada,
and the specifics of the West make Alberta different from the rest of
Canada, to say nothing of the rest of the world. For instance, the contestations over attendance at births in Alberta deviated from the form
common in the rest of Canada, in which (largely male) doctors struggled with (largely female) midwives for legitimacy as accoucheurs. In
Alberta, this struggle was subsumed by the urgent need for any ac-
coucheur at all to attend birthing women scattered across an inhospi-
table terrain. Similarly, the debates over eugenics departed from the
triumphalist rhetoric common in the rest of Canada and in the British
world, taking on what I call the rhetoric of "low" eugenics, in which
sexual sterilization was seen as one imperfect way of partly remediat-
ing the bad behaviour of individual men and women.

The most powerful characteristic shaping "baby trouble," however,
was not the uniqueness of Alberta so much as the enormous stressors
the province faced in its early decades. Although popular histories tend
to portray changes over time as linear progress from a deplorable state
to a better one, Albertans experienced the 1910s, 1920s, and 1930s not as
smooth upward movement but as a cacophony of crises. The real estate
collapse, crop failures, environmental disasters, Spanish flu and other
diseases, war, and the bottom falling out of the agricultural economy all
contributed to a situation in which the making of new people was constantly balanced on a knife-edge between survival and collapse. When
we take reproduction as the central focus of social history, we can see
the precariousness of social and economic life.

This book begins in the early 1900s, when Alberta was becoming a
province, and ends in the 1930s. The Second World War provides an
obvious break point, not only because wars change everything but also
because the era after the war was very different from the prewar years.
Canada and Alberta grew wealthier in the aftermath of the Second
World War. This time of prosperity was marked not just by economic

growth but also by growing pressures towards domestic conformity and social conservatism, as the postwar boom led to the dominance of the "standard North American family" – income-earning father, caregiving mother, joint children living in a single-generation home (Adams 1997; Owram 1997).

After the Second World War, the "baby troubles" of the earlier years receded in favour of a new set of social tensions; these, however, were connected to abundance, leisure, and rapid growth as well as stifling and rigid domestic gender expectations. In Alberta, this abundance was propelled by the first oil boom, inaugurated by the oil well known as Leduc #1 in 1947. Within a very few years, people were pouring into Alberta, and the tide of oil wealth had turned the province into an economic powerhouse with constantly rising, although unequally distributed, individual and household incomes.

What can we finally take away from this account of baby trouble in a particular time and place? The enduring impression left by these episodes is of the passion and precariousness of reproduction. When we move the making of new people to the centre of collective stories, the world looks more dangerous but also more creative and unpredictable. The way we imagine reproduction, and the meanings with which we endow the women, children, and men who are caught up in the making of new people, shape the conditions in which we give birth and are born, as we move our generations forward through time.

Notes

Chapter 1

1 I should be clear here that I am speaking of the biosocial processes of reproduction – conception, pregnancy, childbirth – which produce children.
This is not a book about mothering or parenting in Alberta. Although
chapter 5 does address parenting in the context of discriminating between
"deserving" and "undeserving" mothers, my focus is on the contrast
between normative reproduction – secured within a heterosexual dyad –
and the deviant modes of reproduction that sprang up in the 1910s and
1920s, in which women broke out of, or were removed from, such dyads.

2 In developing this concept, I was particularly inspired the work of Rickie
Solinger (2005, 2000) and Kristin Luker (1975, 1984, 1996, 2006) on the
United States.

3 "Feeble-minded" and "mentally defective" are terms that would not be
used today, because of their offensive connotations. I will follow the conventions of the early twentieth century by not expunging the terms when
they appear in the source material; however, when they appear outside
the context of a direct quote, I will be enclosing them in inverted commas
to signify that they are problematic terms.

Chapter 2

1 During the 1910s and 1920s, women's health, especially reproductive
health, became a focus of agitation and debate across Canada. Women's
bodies, especially in their sexual and reproductive capacities, were debated everywhere as women agitated for political and economic rights. Much
of the rhetoric that had been deployed in contestation over women's right

to the franchise – that women were the makers of nations, who should not be expected to silently suffer the disadvantages of their sex – was also deployed to argue for state support for childbirth. I will not recapitulate the history of the women's movement in Canada, but it is worth noting that arguments about childbirth in Alberta, as with so many other aspects of reproduction, were connected to broader political discussions of women's rights and prerogatives.

2   The *Grain Growers' Guide* deserves particular note. It was founded in Manitoba in 1908 to give a voice to the small farmers who were seeking social and political reform. In 1909 it became the official organ of the United Farmers of Alberta, the Manitoba Grain Growers Association, and the Saskatchewan Grain Growers Association. As such, it covered the prairie provinces, offering a mix of topical news (with a heavy tilt towards prairie populism and collectivism), practical farming advice, and discussions of social and political issues among far-flung farm families. During the 1910s and 1920s, the *Guide*'s women's pages offered recipes and household hints combined with polemics and opinion pieces on pacifism, female suffrage, temperance, and eugenics. Under the editorship of early feminist activist Francis Marion Beynon, these women's pages likely served as most Albertan rural women's introduction to the intricacies of reproductive issues and their salience to the emerging Canadian West.

3   Mitchinson (2002, 170) suggests that such private maternity homes were coming under scrutiny across Canada at that time, especially in Ontario, where concerns were raised about high rates of infant mortality in these "baby farms."

4   The less benign aspects of eugenics are described in detail in chapter 4.

5   This reluctance of new settlers to marry was noted more broadly. An anonymous writer for the *St Albert Star*, in an article titled "Why Do So Many of Our Boys and Girls of Forty Upwards Remain in Single Blessedness," claimed that "comment has often been made upon the number of unmarried men and women ... in western Canada." The author considered placing a tax on male bachelors, decided that would not be effective, and instead recommended that single men and women be educated on the health benefits and lower mortality rates associated with marriage (*St Albert Star*, 24 September 1913, 4).

6   Strangely enough, existing nurses' organizations, such as the Alberta Association of Graduate Nurses, were not involved in lobbying for a district nursing service, and viewed the service as a potential source of competition. The graduate nurses were especially concerned that semi-trained midwives

would be deployed as district nurses rather than trained "graduate nurses." Many graduate nurses believed that the emphasis on childbirth that animated the creation of the district nursing service would degrade the reputation of nursing by equating them with "mere" midwives (Ross-Kerr 1998, 95–6).

Chapter 3

1   This idea of multiple economies of reproduction is indebted to Pierre Bourdieu's idea of multiple convertible forms of capital (Bourdieu 1986); however, the concept of capital, even fungible capital, is insufficient to represent the dynamics of accumulation, depletion, investment, and valuation in which Beulah was imbricated.

2   While the scrapbooks contain many newspaper articles about Beulah, the scrapbook keepers were not always scrupulous about dating the clippings. I thus infer the year or month of publication based on the clipping's location in the chronological order of the scrapbooks.

3   PAA stands for "Provincial Archives of Alberta."

4   The annual "open day," usually held on the anniversary of Beulah's move to 137th Avenue, became a major fundraising and public relations event. Newspapers published stories and features leading up to the open day, cars were hired to transport visitors without their own transportation out to the home, tea was served, and the program featured inspirational speakers from Beulah and the broader evangelical community. The high point of the open day was a tour of the home, including the specially decorated nurseries full of well-scrubbed and charming babies.

5   Beulah was formally non-denominational, although in practice it was ecumenically Protestant. Potential clients who were Catholic were encouraged to seek out the services of a home run by the Sisters of the Misericord in Edmonton. During the board of directors meeting of 9 January 1934, concern was expressed about "the admission of Catholic girls, and it was agreed that their coming should be curtailed" (PAA 93.359, Beulah Home minutes). No information is available about clients of Eastern Orthodox background, the other major Christian religious grouping in Edmonton, although the recruitment and retention of staff who could speak Ukrainian suggests that they were considered acceptable clients.

6   It is also possible that Aboriginal women who sought an institutional home when they became pregnant outside of marriage may have gone to the Sisters of the Misericord, who also operated a maternity home,

because of the influence of the Catholic Church in Aboriginal communities. However, I was unable to find any information about this home.

7 The time was ripe for concerns about baby-selling, in the wake of the scandals surrounding the Ideal Maternity Home in Nova Scotia, where babies were openly sold to American would-be parents for upwards of $1,000, while the biological mother was told her baby had died. Many unmarketable babies were neglected by the staff and died.

Chapter 4

1 Puplampu (2008) argues that University of Alberta psychology professor John MacEachran, who chaired the Sexual Sterilization Committee for decades, comes close to being the intellectual voice of the movement; however, MacEachran's writings are not particularly original.

2 I will follow the convention of the early twentieth century in using terms like "feeble-minded" and "defective." I realize that these words are offensive today. However, there is no precise lexical equivalent for the social category referred to as the "feeble-minded" or the "defective," as these terms do not map onto the category of people who would today be referred to as intellectually challenged or developmentally disabled. The early-twentieth-century terms designate a much wider category of people who were considered erratic, incomprehensible or uncontrollable, as well as those who were considered mentally "slow."

3 The apogee of this passion for ordering the gendered world through maternal feminism may have been reached at their 1922 convention, at which a resolution was brought forward requesting that the UFWA go on record as disapproving of long skirts and requiring that skirts be at least seven inches from the ground and of sufficient width as to be modest and graceful. Various locals at different times also requested that resolutions on neckline depth and the minimum amount of material needed to make a socially acceptable decent dress be considered.

4 In those years the association of eugenics with women was set, to the extent that the guide published an extended satirical story about a world in which "eugenist suffragettes" had taken over England and the United States and were busy inverting the political and economic gender order. These "eugenist suffragettes" were also depicted as chasing handsome young men through the streets to capture them and marry them off, in order to ensure "scientific propagation" ("Pro Bono Publico," *Grain Growers Guide*, 20 March 1912).

Chapter 5

1   The federal Canadian state was almost entirely irrelevant to the question
of mothers' allowances. The salient levels of state power here are the
province and the municipality or district.

2   The City of Edmonton Board of Public Welfare engaged in running
skirmishes with the province in the 1920s over the question of whether
"proven immorality" should be grounds for removing a recipient. It went
so far as to request that the mayor of Edmonton meet with the premier
so as to lay out the argument for cutting off mothers who consorted with
men to whom they were not married. The question of immorality –
proven, unproven, or suspected – and its relationship to women's fitness
for the precious work of social reproduction was a vexed one (see below).

3   Interestingly, although the Alberta of those decades was an intensely xenophobic environment, the archival traces of the mothers' allowance program do not suggest that ethnic origin played a role in shaping which
mothers received support and which did not. In the City of Edmonton
archives, correspondence and case files related to *men* who sought support
as a result of unemployment or other crises are peppered with annotations
about the ethnic characteristics these men supposedly displayed, such as
an aversion to honest work or a tendency towards drunkenness and
aggression. The city even contemplated cutting off all support to men
of German or Austrian backgrounds during the First World War, on the
grounds that providing food, fuel, or money was in effect supporting
the enemy.

4   However, when it came to women of the same backgrounds (judging by
surnames), such commentary and arbitrary decisions about granting support were absent, suggesting that somehow the very fact of being a mother
in need overrode problematic ethnic identities. Women who applied for
support were subjected to investigation to determine whether they were
efficient housekeepers and whether their children's behaviour testified to
their effectiveness as mothers, but if they were able to meet this scrutiny,
their work in raising new citizens for the city and the province exempted
them from the sort of hostile xenophobia directed at their male counterparts by the predominantly Anglo-Saxon burghers of Edmonton.

References

Abramovitz, M. 1996. *Regulating the Lives of Women: Social Welfare Policy from Colonial Times to the Present*. Boston: South End Press.

Adams, Mary Louise. 1997. *The Trouble with Normal: Postwar Youth and the Making of Heterosexuality*. Toronto: University of Toronto Press.

Adams, M.B. 1990. *The Wellborn Science: Eugenics in Germany, France, Brazil, and Russia*. Oxford: Oxford University Press.

Allen, Garland E. 1986. "The Eugenics Record Office at Cold Spring Harbour 1910–1940: An Essay in Institutional History." *Osiris* 2: 225–64. http://dx.doi.org/10.1086/368657.

Arnup, Catherine. 1994. *Education for Motherhood: Advice for Mothers in Twentieth-Century Canada*. Toronto: University of Toronto Press.

Baillargeon, Denyse. 2009. *Babies for the Nation: The Medicalization of Motherhood in Quebec*. Waterloo: Wilfrid Laurier University Press.

Barrett, Deborah, and Charles Kurzman. 2004. "Globalizing Social Movement Theory: The Case of Eugenics." *Theory and Society* 33(5): 487–527. http://dx.doi.org/10.1023/B:RYSO.0000045719.45687.aa.

Bashford, A., & P. Levine, eds. 2010. *The Oxford Handbook of the History of Eugenics*. Oxford: Oxford University Press.

Bayat-Rizi, Zohreh. 2008. "From Fate to Risk: The Quantification of Mortality in Early Modern Statistics." *Theory, Culture, & Society* 25(1): 121–43. http://dx.doi.org/10.1177/0263276407085160.

Bezanson, Kate, and Meg Luxton, eds. 2006. *Social Reproduction: Feminist Politics Challenges Neoliberalism*. Montreal: McGill-Queen's University Press.

Black, Edwin. 2003. *War against the Weak: Eugenics and America's Campaign to Create a Master Race*. New York: Thunder's Mouth Press.

Bledsoe, Caroline. 2002. *Contingent Lives: Fertility, Time, and Aging in West Africa*. Chicago: University of Chicago Press.

Bledsoe, C.H., A.G. Hill, U. d'Alessandro, and P. Langerock. 1994. "Construct-ing Natural Fertility: The Use of Western Contraceptive Technologies in Rural Gambia." *Population and Development Review* 20(1): 81–113.

Bourdieu, Pierre. 1986. "The Forms of Capital." In *Handbook of Theory of Research for the Sociology of Education*, ed. J.E. Richards, 241–58. New York: Greenwood Press.

Bright, D. 2005. "A Year of Extraordinary Difficulty: 1919." In *Alberta Formed, Alberta Transformed*, ed. C. Cavanaugh, D. Weatherell, and M. Payne. Edmonton: University of Alberta Press.

Browner, Carol. 2000. "Situating Women's Reproductive Activities." *American Anthropologist* 102(4): 773–88. http://dx.doi.org/10.1525/aa.2000.102.4.773.

Brush, Lisa D. 1997. "Worthy Widows, Welfare Cheats: Proper Womanhood in Expert Needs Talk about Single Mothers in the United States, 1900 to 1988." *Gender & Society* 11(6): 720–46. http://dx.doi.org/10.1177/089124397011006002.

Burnett, Kristin. 2010. *Taking Medicine: Women's Healing Work and Colonial Contact in Southern Alberta, 1880–1930*. Vancouver: UBC Press.

Cairney, Richard. 1996. "'Democracy Was Never Intended for Degenerates': Alberta's Flirtation with Eugenics Comes Back to Haunt It." *Canadian Medical Association Journal* 155: 489–92.

Carter, Sarah. 2008. *The Importance of Being Monogamous: Marriage and Nation Building in Western Canada to 1915*. Edmonton: University of Alberta Press.

Caulfield, Timothy, and Gerald Robertson. 1996. "Eugenic Policies in Alberta: From the Systematic to the Systemic?" *Alberta Law Review* 35: 59–79.

Cavanaugh, Catherine. 1993. "The Limits of the Pioneering Partnership: The Alberta Campaign for Homestead Dower, 1909–25." *Canadian Historical Review* 74(2): 198–225. http://dx.doi.org/10.3138/CHR-074-02-02.

Cavanaugh, Catherine. 1997. "No Place for a Woman: Engendering Western Canadian Settlement." *Western Historical Quarterly* 28(4): 493–518. http://dx.doi.org/10.2307/969883.

Cavanaugh, C., D. Weatherell, and M. Payne. 2006. *Alberta Formed, Alberta Transformed*. Edmonton: University of Alberta Press.

Chambers, Lori. 2007. *Misconceptions: Unmarried Motherhood and the Ontario Children of Unmarried Parents Act, 1921–1969*. Toronto: University of Toronto Press.

Chapman, T. 1977. "Early Eugenics Movement in Western Canada." *Alberta History* 25(4): 9–17.

Christian, T. 1974. "The Mentally Ill and Human Rights in Alberta: A Study of the Alberta Sexual Sterilization Act." Unpublished research report, Faculty of Law, University of Alberta.

Colen, S. 1990. "Housekeeping for the Green Card: West Indian Household Workers, the State, and Stratified Reproduction in New York." *At Work in Homes: Household Workers in World Perspective* 3: 89–118.

Comacchio, Cynthia. 1993. *Nations Are Built of Babies: Saving Ontario's Mothers and Children, 1900–1940*. Montreal: McGill-Queen's University Press.

Connell, R.W. 1998. "Masculinities and globalization." *Men and Masculinities*, 1(1): 3–23.

Corbett, Elise Elliott. 1979. "Alberta Women in the 1920s: An Inquiry into Four Aspects of Their Lives." MA thesis, University of Calgary.

Cran, M. 1910. *A Woman in Canada*. Philadelphia: J.B. Lippincott Company; London: J. Milne.

Davin, Anna. 1978. "Imperialism and Motherhood." *History Workshop* 5(1): 9–66. http://dx.doi.org/10.1093/hwj/5.1.9.

Dowbiggin, Ian. 1997. *Keeping America Sane: Psychiatry and Eugenics in the United States and Canada, 1880–1940*. Ithaca: Cornell University Press.

Dyck, Erika. 2013. *Facing Eugenics: Reproduction, Sterilization, and the Politics of Choice*. Toronto: University of Toronto Press.

Elliott, George. 1911. "What Courses in Social Science, Pure or Applied, Should Be Included in Household Departments of Applied Science?" *Journal of Home Economics* 3: 33–49.

Engels, Friedrich. 1972. *The Origin of the Family, Private Property, and the State*. New York: International Publishers.

Friedman, Helen L. 1975. "Why Are They Keeping Their Babies?" *Social Work* 20(4): 322.

Frohman, Larry. 2006. "Welfare and Citizenship: The War on Tuberculosis and Infant Mortality in Germany, 1900–1930." *Central European History* 39(3): 431–81. http://dx.doi.org/10.1017/S000893890600015X.

Gal, Susan, and Gail Kligman, eds. 2000. *Reproducing Gender: Politics, Publics, and Everyday Life after Socialism*. Princeton: Princeton University Press.

Garrett, Paul M. 2000. "The Abnormal Flight: The Migration and Repatriation of Irish Unmarried Mothers." *Social History* 25(3): 330–43. http://dx.doi.org/10.1080/03071020050143356.

Ginsburg, Faye, and Rayna Rapp. 1991. "The Politics of Reproduction." *Annual Review of Anthropology* 20: 311–43.

Ginsburg, Faye, and Rayna Rapp, eds. 1995. *Conceiving the New World Order: The Global Politics of Reproduction*. Berkeley: University of California Press.

Gordon, L. 1994. *Pitied but Not Entitled: Single Mothers and the History of Welfare, 1890–1935*. New York: The Free Press.

Gould, Stephen J. 1981. *The Mismeasure of Man*. New York: W.W. Norton.

Greenhalgh, S. 2008. *Just One Child: Science and Policy in Deng's China*. Berkeley: University of California Press.

Greenhalgh, Susan, ed. 1995. *Situating Fertility: Anthropology and Demographic Inquiry*. Cambridge: Cambridge University Press. http://dx.doi.org/10.1017/CBO9780511621611.

Greenhalgh, Susan, and J. Li. 1995. "Engendering Reproductive Policy and Practice in Peasant China: For a Feminist Demography of Reproduction." *Signs* 20(3): 601–33. http://dx.doi.org/10.1086/495002.

Grekul, Jana. 2002. "The Social Construction of the Feebleminded Threat: Implementation of the Sexual Sterilization Act in Alberta, 1929–1972." PhD diss., University of Alberta.

Grekul, Jana. 2008. "Sterilization in Alberta, 1928–1972: Gender Matters." *Canadian Review of Sociology* 45(3): 247–67. http://dx.doi.org/10.1111/j.1755-618X.2008.00014.x.

Grekul, Jana, Harvey Krahn, and Dave Odynak. 2004. "Sterilizing the 'Feeble-Minded': Eugenics in Alberta, Canada, 1929–1972." *Journal of Historical Sociology* 17(4): 358–84. http://dx.doi.org/10.1111/j.1467-6443.2004.00237.x.

Hiroko, Takeda. 2004. *The Political Economy of Reproduction in Japan*: London: Routledge.

Jasen, Patricia. 1997. "Race, Culture, and the Colonization of Childbirth in Northern Canada." *Social History of Medicine* 10(3): 383–400. http://dx.doi.org/10.1093/shm/10.3.383.

Jenson, Jane, and Mariette Simeau, eds. 2003. *Who Cares: Women's Work, Childcare, and Welfare State Redesign*. Toronto: University of Toronto Press.

Jones, D. 2005. "The Dance of the Grizzly Bear: From Boom to Bust, 1912–1913." In *Alberta Formed, Alberta Transformed*, ed. C. Cavanaugh, D. Weatherell, and M. Payne, 360–85. Edmonton: University of Alberta Press.

Kaler, Amy. 2000. "'Who Has Told You to Do This Thing?' Towards a Feminist Interpretation of Contraceptive Diffusion in Rhodesia, 1970–1980." *Signs* 25(3): 677–708. http://dx.doi.org/10.1086/495478.

Kaler, Amy. 2004. *Running After Pills: Gender, Politics, and Contraception in Colonial Rhodesia*. Portsmouth: Heinenmann Press.

Kaaneh, Rhoda Ann. 2002. *Birthing the Nation: Strategies of Palestinian Women in Israel*. Berkeley: University of California Press.

Kandaswamy, P. 2010. "'You Trade In a Man for the Man': Domestic Violence and the US Welfare State." *American Quarterly* 62(2): 253–77.

Kaufman, Sharon, and Lynn Morgan. 2005. "The Anthropology of the Beginnings and Endings of Life." *Annual Review of Anthropology* 34(1): 317–41. http://dx.doi.org/10.1146/annurev.anthro.34.081804.120452.

Kellogg, J.H. 1914. "Needed: A New Human Race." In *Official Proceedings*, vol. 1: *Proceedings of the First National Conference on Race Betterment*, ed. Emily F. Robbins, 431–50. Battle Creek: Race Betterment Foundation.

Kligman, Gail. 1998. *The Politics of Duplicity: Controlling Reproduction in Ceausescu's Romania*. Berkeley: University of California Press.

Kline, Wendy. 2001. *Building a Better Race: Gender, Sexuality, and Eugenics from the Turn of the Century to the Baby Boom*. Berkeley: University of California Press.

Kunzel, Regina G. 1988. "The Professionalization of Benevolence: Evangelicals and Social Workers in the Florence Crittenton Homes, 1915 to 1945." *Journal of Social History* 22(1): 21–43. http://dx.doi.org/10.1353/jsh/22.1.21.

Kunzel, R.G. 1995. *Fallen Women, Problem Girls: Unmarried Mothers and the Professionalization of Social Work, 1890–1945*. New Haven: Yale University Press.

Langford, Nanci. 1995. "Childbirth on the Canadian Prairies." *Journal of Historical Sociology* 8(3): 278–302. http://dx.doi.org/10.1111/j.1467-6443.1995.tb00090.x.

Levesque, Andree. 1994. *Making and Breaking the Rules: Women in Quebec, 1919–1939*, trans. Yvonne Klein. Toronto: McClelland & Stewart.

Little, Margaret Jane Hillyard. 1998. *No Car, No Radio, No Liquor Permit: The Moral Regulation of Single Mothers in Ontario, 1920–1997*. Toronto: Oxford University Press.

Luddy, Maria. 2011. "Unmarried Mothers in Ireland, 1880–1973." *Women's History Review* 20(1): 109–26. http://dx.doi.org/10.1080/09612025.2011.536393.

Luker, K. 1975. *Taking Chances: Abortion and the Decision Not to Contracept*. Berkeley: University of California Press

Luker, K. 1984. *Abortion and the Politics of Motherhood*. Berkeley: University of California Press.

Luker, K. 1996. *Dubious Conceptions: The Politics of Teenage Pregnancy*. Harvard University Press.

Luker, K. 2006. *When Sex Goes to School: Warring Views on Sex and Sex Education since the Sixties*. New York: W.W. Norton.

Luxton, Meg. 1980. *More Than a Labor of Love: Three Generations of Women's Work in the Home*. Toronto: Women's Press.

Luxton, Meg. 2006. "Feminist Political Economy and Social Reproduction." In *Social Reproduction: Feminist Politics Challenges Neoliberalism*, ed. Kate Bezanson and Meg Luxton, 1–44. Montreal: McGill-Queen's University Press.

MacMurchy, Helen. 1924. *Maternal Mortality in Canada*. Ottawa: Government Press.

MacMurchy, Helen. 1925. "On Maternal Mortality in Canada." *Canadian Medical Association Journal* 15(3): 293–7.

McClung, Nellie. 1945. *The Stream Runs Fast: My Own Story*. Toronto: Thomas Allen.

McDaniel, Susan. 1996. "Toward a Synthesis of Feminist and Demographic Perspectives on Fertility." *Sociological Quarterly* 37: 83–104.

McGregar, D. 1917. *The Alberta Club Woman's Blue Book*. Calgary: Canadian Women's Press Club.

McLaren, Angus. 1990. *Our Own Master Race: Eugenics in Canada, 1885–1945*. Toronto: McClelland & Stewart.

McPhail, E. Stuart. 1927. "Infant Mortality as Shown by Canadian Vital Statistics." *American Journal of Public Health* 17(5): 476–84. http://dx.doi.org/10.2105/AJPH.17.5.476.

Mitchinson, Wendy. 2002. *Giving Birth in Canada 1900–1950*. Toronto: University of Toronto Press.

Murray, Karen Bridget. 2004. "Governing 'Unwed Mothers' In Toronto at the Turn of the Twentieth Century." *Canadian Historical Review* 85(2): 253–76.

Ordover, Nancy. 2003. *American Eugenics: Race, Queer Anatomy, and the Science of Nationalism*. Minneapolis: University of Minnesota Press.

Orloff, A. 1996. "Gender in the Welfare State." *Annual Review of Sociology*, 51–78.

Owram, Doug. 1997. *Born at the Right Time: A History of the Baby Boom Generation*. Toronto: University of Toronto Press.

Paxson, Heather. 2004. *Making Modern Mothers: Ethics and Family Planning in Urban Greece*. Berkeley: University of California Press.

Petrie, Ann. 1998. *Gone to an Aunt's: Remembering Canada's Home for Unwed Mothers*. Toronto: McClelland & Stewart.

Puplampu, Korbla. 2008. "Knowledge, Power, and Social Policy: John M. MacEachran and Alberta's 1928 Sexual Sterilization Act." *Alberta Journal of Educational Research* 54(2): 129–46.

Rafter, Nicole Hahn. 1988a. *White Trash: The Eugenic Family Studies, 1887–1919*. Boston: Northeastern University Press.

Rafter, Nicole Hahn. 1988b. "White Trash: Eugenics as Social Ideology." *Society* 26(1): 43–9. http://dx.doi.org/10.1007/BF02698315.

Rains, Prudence M. 1970. "Moral Reinstatement." *American Behavioral Scientist* 14(2): 219–35. http://dx.doi.org/10.1177/000276427001400205.

Rapp, Rayna. 2001. "Gender, Body, Biomedicine: How Some Feminist Concerns Dragged Reproduction to the Center of Social Theory." *Medical Anthropology Quarterly* 15(4): 466–77. http://dx.doi.org/10.1525/maq.2001.15.4.466.

Reeves, Josephine. 1993. "The Deviant Mother and Child: The Development of Adoption as an Instrument of Social Control." *Journal of Law and Society* 20(4): 412–26. http://dx.doi.org/10.2307/1410209.

Relyea, M. Joyce. 1992. "The Rebirth of Midwifery in Canada: An Historical Perspective." *Midwifery* 8(4): 159–69. http://dx.doi.org/10.1016/S0266-6138(05)80002-6.

Renne, E.P. 2003. *Population and Progress in a Yoruba Town*. Ann Arbor: University of Michigan Press.

Rennie, Bradford James. 2000. *The Rise of Agrarian Democracy: The United Farmers and Farm Women of Alberta, 1909–1921*. Toronto: University of Toronto Press.

Rennie, Bradford James. 2005. "From Idealism to Pragmatism: 1923 in Alberta." In *Alberta Formed, Alberta Transformed*, ed. C. Cavanaugh, D. Weatherell, and M. Payne. Edmonton: University of Alberta Press.

Richardson, George. 1918. *Homesteading: Two Prairie Seasons*. London: T. Fisher Unwin.

Richardson, Sharon. 1995. "Frontier Nursing: Nursing Work and Training in Alberta, 1890–1905." *Canadian Journal of Nursing Research* 28(3): 113–40.

Riley, N.E. 1999. "Challenging Demography: Contributions from Feminist Theory." *Sociological Forum* 14(3): pp. 369–397.

Roseneil, Sasha, Isabel Crowhurst, Ana Cristina Santos, and Mariya Stoilova. 2013. "Reproduction and Citizenship/Reproducing Citizens." *Citizenship Studies* 17(8): 901–11. http://dx.doi.org/10.1080/13621025.2013.851067.

Ross-Kerr, Janet. 1998. *Prepared to Care: Nurses and Nursing in Alberta*. Edmonton: University of Alberta Press.

Scheper-Hughes, Nancy. 1993. *Death without Weeping: The Violence of Everyday Life in Brazil*. Berkeley: University of California Press.

Schneider, Jane. 1996. *Festival of the Poor: Fertility Decline and the Ideology of Class in Sicily, 1860–1980*. Tucson: University of Arizona Press.

Schoen, Joanna. 2005. *Choice and Coercion: Birth Control, Sterilization and Abortion in Public Health and Welfare*. Chapel Hill: University of North Carolina Press.

Selden, Steven. 2005. "Transforming Better Babies into Fitter Families: Archival Resources and the History of the American Eugenics Movement." *Proceedings of the American Philosophical Society* 149(2): 199–225.

Silverman, Eliane Laslau. 1998. *The Last Best West: Women on the Alberta Frontier, 1890–1930*. Calgary: Fifth House Publishers.

Smith, Dorothy. 1999. *Writing the Social: Critique, Theory, and Investigations*. Toronto: University of Toronto Press.

Solinger, R. 2005. *Pregnancy and Power: A Short History of Reproductive Politics in America*. New York: New York University Press.

Solinger, Rickie. 2000. *Wake Up Little Susie: Single Pregnancy and Race before Roe v. Wade*, 2nd ed. New York: Routledge.

Spensky, M. 1992. "Producers of Legitimacy: Homes for Unmarried Mothers in the 1950s." In *Regulating Motherhood: Historical Essays on Marriage, Motherhood, and Sexuality*, ed. Carol Smart, 100–18. London: Routledge.

Statistics Canada. 1976. Historical Statistics of Canada: Section B, Vital Statistics and Health. http://www.statcan.gc.ca/pub/11-516-x/sectionb/4147437-eng.htm#cont.

Stewart, Irene. 1979. *These Were Our Yesterdays: A History of District Nursing in Alberta*. Edmonton: D.W. Friesen & Sons.

Stoler, Ann, and Frederick Cooper. 1995. *Race and the Education of Desire: Foucault's History of Sexuality and the Colonial Order of Things*. Durham: Duke University Press.

Strange, Carolyn. 1995. *Toronto's Girl Problem: The Perils and Pleasures of the City, 1880–1930*. Toronto: University of Toronto Press.

Strong-Boag, Veronica. 2006. *Finding Family, Finding Ourselves: English Canada Encounters Adoption from the Nineteenth Century to the 1990s*. Toronto: Oxford University Press.

Strong-Boag, Veronica. 2011. *Fostering Nation? Canada Confronts the History of Childhood Disadvantage*. Waterloo: Wilfrid Laurier University Press.

Taylor, Charles. 2002. "Modern Social Imaginaries." *Public Culture* 14(1): 91–124. http://dx.doi.org/10.1215/08992363-14-1-91.

Thane, Pat. 2011. "Unmarried Motherhood in Twentieth-Century England." *Women's History Review* 20(1): 11–29. http://dx.doi.org/10.1080/09612025.2011.536383.

Titmuss, Richard. 1943. *Birth, Poverty, and Wealth: A Study of Infant Mortality*. London: Hamish Hamilton Medical Books.

Valverde, Mariana. 2008. *The Age of Light, Soap, and Water: Moral Reform in English Canada, 1885–1925*. Toronto: University of Toronto Press.

Van Herk, A. 2010. *Mavericks: An Incorrigible History Of Alberta*. Toronto: Penguin Canada.

Vant, J. Ross, and Tony Cashman. 1986. *More Than a Hospital: University of Alberta Hospitals, 1906–1986*. Edmonton: University Hospitals Board.

Vincent, C.E. 1960. "Unmarried Fathers and the Mores: 'Sexual Exploiter' as an Ex Post Facto Label." *American Sociological Review* 25(1): 40–6.

Vosko, L. 2002. "The Pasts (and Futures) of Canadian Feminist Political Economy: Reviving the Debate." *Studies in Political Economy* 68: 55–82.

Wahlsten, Douglas. 1997. "Leilani Muir versus the Philosopher King: Eugenics on Trial in Alberta." *Genetica* 99(2–3): 185–98. http://dx.doi.org/10.1007/BF02259522.

Weir, Lorna. 2006. *Pregnancy, Risk, and Biopolitics: On the Threshold of the Living Subject*. New York: Routledge.

West, E. 1918. *Homesteading: Two Prairie Seasons*. London: T.F. Unwin.

Wetherell, Donald G. 2005. "Making New Identities: Alberta's Small Towns Confront the City, 1900–1950." *Journal of Canadian Studies / Revue d'Etudes Canadiennes* 39(1): 175–97.

Wetherell, Donald, and Irene Kmet. 1995. *Town Life: Main Street and the Evolution of Small Town Alberta, 1880–1947*. Edmonton: University of Alberta Press.

Woods, R.I., P.A. Patterson, and J.H. Woodward. 2010. "The Causes of Rapid Infant Mortality Decline in England and Wales, 1861–1921, Part 1." *Population Studies* 42(3): 343–66. http://dx.doi.org/10.1080/0032472031000143516.

Yuval-Davis, Nira. 1997. *Gender and Nation*. London: Cambridge University Press.

Yuval-Davis, Nira, and Floya Anthias, eds. 1989. *Woman–Nation–State*. New York: Macmillan. http://dx.doi.org/10.1007/978-1-349-19865-8.

Index